DOWNRIVER

Currents of Style in Louisiana Painting 1800-1950

Alfred L. Boisseau (born France, 1823-1901)
Miss Tanner, Warbon Plantation, 1849
oil on canvas
39 1/2 x 32 inches
James D. Didier Collection

DOWNRIVER

Currents of Style in Louisiana Painting 1800-1950

Estill Curtis Pennington
Adjunct Curator of American Art
New Orleans Museum of Art

Pelican Publishing Company
GRETNA 1991

Library of Congress Cataloging-in-Publication Data

Pennington, Estill Curtis.
Downriver : currents of style in Louisiana painting, 1800-1950 /Estill Curtis Pennington.
p. cm.
Includes bibliographical references.
ISBN 0-88289-800-0
1. Painting, American—Louisiana. 2. Painting, Modern—19th century—Louisiana. 3. Painting, Modern—20th century—Louisiana.
I. Title.
ND230.L8P46 1990
759.163—dc20 90-6932
CIP

This book has been produced under the auspices of the New Orleans Museum of Art.

Manufactured in Hong Kong
Published by Pelican Publishing Company, Inc.
1101 Monroe Street, Gretna, Louisiana 70053

CONTENTS

Josephine Marien Crawford (1878-1952)
Her First Communion, 1935
oil on canvas
39 x 24 inches
Mr. and Mrs. Richard B. Kaufmann Collection

PREFACE
Currents of Style

THE IMPRESSIVE ARRAY OF painting created in Louisiana between 1800 and 1950 offers the art historian one of the most substantial bodies of material culture for stylistic analysis in the canon of Southern studies. That this material culture was created against a background of social and economic life which parallels, and even expands upon, certain consistent themes in the national culture is even more exciting.

However, from the outset, it should be noted that this volume is indeed a study of style which departs from traditional considerations of art created in the South. To this point Southern art studies have been under the enormous burden of gathering primary material, creating catalogs of artists' works, and bringing this work to the attention of the public. The exhibition *Painting in the South: 1564-1980,* which was organized by the Virginia Museum in 1983 and travelled to Southern museums for two years, was the most important development in Southern art studies to date, but it was only a beginning, indeed a challenge to subsequent efforts.

That challenge has been well met, and in great depth, by several institutions in Louisiana. The Historic New Orleans Collection's *Encyclopedia of New Orleans Artists 1718-1918* is now the definitive source for biographical material on artists working in the area. Acquisition efforts of the Louisiana State Museum, the New Orleans Museum of Art and the Anglo-American Museum have resulted in public collections which ensure the survival of a large group of works by a varied cross-sampling of the artists working in Louisiana.

Fortunately, several noted collectors of Louisiana painting have also contributed to the possibility for study. Early in this century, at the point of lowest interest, Isaac Monroe Cline assembled an impressive group of Louisiana paintings from the nineteenth century. Albert Lieutaud's shop on Royal Street in the Vieux Carré was a point of transit for many excellent works. In more recent years, William E. Groves, Dr. and Mrs. James Nelson, the White family, Ray and Martha Ann Samuel, and Roger Houston Ogden have put together enviable collections of works by the most outstanding artists. Mr. Ogden, in particular, has been an inspired participant in this venture.

While it should never be stated that the important task of locating additional works by known artists, and continuing the search for works by little-known artists, should cease, more pressing considerations in the study of all Southern art persist. Every successful retrieval by the cultural archeologist of Southern painting renews the need for interpretations of the type which have been created in other fields of American art. Whether or not Southern art requires a Southern point of view is a rather involved topic which I have explored in my previous book.[1] Whether Southern paintings in general or Louisiana paintings in particular have been excluded from larger American art studies by willfulness or neglect is one of the situations which both this volume and the exhibition it complements seek to address. "Downriver: Currents of Style in Louisiana Painting" was organized as the Odyssey Ball exhibition by the New Orleans Museum of Art in 1990.

As a methodological and literary source, one of the most influential interpretive studies of American art is Barbara Novak's *American Painting of the Nineteenth Century*. In her preface to that work, Professor Novak defines her goals as twofold: "to isolate more specifically certain characteristics in American art that we can with some degree of confidence denote as American" and to compose essays "intended to establish a perspective of ideas against which some of the more important American artists of the nineteenth century can be studied."[2]

Both of these goals are fulfilled in a brilliant volume which provides, as do subsequent writings by John Wilmerding, Wendell Garret, and Theodore Stebbins, guidelines for defining the "perspective of ideas" against which various artists in Louisiana functioned. The fundamental purpose of this study is to examine the extent to which the functioning artistic community of Louisiana absorbed national themes and trends, which we can see manifested in the style and content of Louisiana painting.

Historically, American art studies have concentrated on the similarities and distinctions between American and European styles, an interaction which Novak terms a "process of transformation." This transformation is expanded in Louisiana because of its entrenched, non-English-speaking colonial culture which neither sought independence from a mother culture through armed rebellion nor participated in the self-conscious effort to create a new national identity.

Like most of the country which joined the union after the original thirteen colonies, Louisiana had an indigenous culture and society. In the case of Louisiana, however, this culture was one of the strongest ones to be grafted onto the nation state, even as it retained most of its existing social and economic structure and ethnic imperative. We have an unfortunate tendency in this country to view all cultural developments through the Federal lens. This is a most inadequate vantage for seeing a culture as established and complex as that of Louisiana. By a marvellous irony, it may well be that the traditional Southern reluctance to be considered by national values rather than local options serves the study of Southern painting quite well when these objects are given a formal analysis.

Novak's dialectic charts the interaction of the European tradition with an American art which she defines—either by design or default—as entirely that of the northeast. In Louisiana that same interaction exists, pulsing with a vibrancy which was renewed with each new wave of itinerant artists arriving upon the scene.

"Currents of style" is a deliberate subtitle intended to function as an extended metaphor for this study. The presence of the Mississippi River and the proximity of the Gulf of Mexico were the mainstream sources for the implicit fluidity of Louisiana life. "Currents" is also a useful metaphor for compositional approaches, technical means, and instructional resources available to the practicing artist in Louisiana.

The study of style in art is the most provocative pursuit the art historian can undertake. When considering style it is well to recall Erwin Panofsky's lament that the lack of interest in the study of exact proportion in art is due to an "indifference...explained by the modern subjective viewpoint that a work of art is something utterly irrational."[3] Panofsky points out that the "modern spectator, still under the influence of...Romantic interpretation of art, finds it uninteresting, if not distressing, when the historian tells him that a rational system...underlies this or that representation."

Panofsky's observation rings true across a wide range of art studies. Lurking within the popular consciousness of art is a suspicion that linking the work of one artist with that of another, especially in an effort to demonstrate either influence or verisimilitude of detail, is somehow demeaning to the act of creativity itself. In our own time, this suspicion has been bulwarked by repeated insistence in the contemporary art world since the Second World War that each new work of art is unlike anything which preceded it. This has resulted in an art aesthetic which relentlessly pursues the novel at the expense of worthy, established traditions of style.

Ultimately, "style" is one way of comprehending what an art object looks like and why it was created in that manner. Novak's concept of a "perspective of ideas" enlivens the study of style when positive, well-thought-out associations, both implicit and historical, can be drawn between artists and their works. Thus, Gilbert Stuart's conversations with Matthew Harris Jouett in Boston on portrait compositional conventions takes on an entirely new significance when considered as a source for the introduction of Federal neoclassicism into the world of Louisiana portraiture, which had previously been dominated by the canons of Spanish colonialism as practiced by the enigmatic Salazar.

While the creation of a "perspective of ideas" on stylistic development in Louisiana painting is the principal goal of this study, other currents will surge into the mainstream as well. Without any intention of diminishing the creation of any individual work of art, it cannot be imagined that paintings are created in a vacuum, divorced from either market concerns or social issues. On the other hand, it would hardly be either fair or helpful to create a study of painting that significantly diverged from a certain historical consensus. No effort is being made here to impose schools or create movements that did not exist. For the most part, the art that is being examined falls into those same basic categories of portraiture, landscape, genre painting, and nonrepresentationalism with which the informed viewer is familiar.

The public is most familiar with the portraiture and landscape art of the mid-nineteenth century, for these are the forms of art which have created the most evocative images of historical figures and exotic locales. The most disparaged form of Louisiana painting was created immediately following this period, the academic art of the late nineteenth century which often has a curious, inaccessible style, and a content which has been dated by its all too close association with social attitudes which are now in eclipse.

On the other hand, the most acclaimed period of Louisiana art, both in the contemporary market place and public awareness, is the art of the Woodward Brothers and the Newcomb School of potters. By contrast, the efforts of the Louisiana modernists remain virtually unknown, though the same responses to prevailing trends which can be identified in earlier periods may be seen in much of this work.

However, in one area of subject matter, this study does indeed attempt to create a new critical, and interpretive, framework. Much of the genre painting in the 100-year period between 1850 and 1950, spanning slavery and the rise of the civil rights movement, uses the black figure as a vehicle for expressing an ofttimes hidden, ofttimes flagrant political and social agenda. The widespread popularity of this art in its own day, the technical excellence of the artists who created it, and the current marketability of such works make it an art form which cannot be ignored. By identifying parallel events in the history of blacks in Louisiana with the subject matter in these works, it is to be hoped that a more objective understanding of them may be reached.

While lofty points of connoisseurship may not be well served by this study, the richness of material culture in the region must be recognized. Louisiana has the most substantial, extensive, and certainly the most profoundly ongoing plastic arts tradition in the South, and rivals major northeastern centers for consistency in output, if not in excellence. One is often tempted to reach conclusions where none are called for, and to avoid stating those conclusions which one would rather deny. Increasing an awareness of Louisiana painting may prompt some unfortunate comparisons with the works of other American artists, but the greater canvas will not be ill served in the process.

Throughout the course of research on this volume I was aware that the absence of any really extensive primary materials would be gravely regretted. One always yearns to know what the artist was thinking, or feeling, in the course of creating works of art. Few letters or journals have been found, but there are some consistent, and recurring, voices. By and large what we know about both art and artists in Louisiana is what has appeared in popular journals and newspapers of the day. Perhaps this serves a study of style quite well, for it at least provides a contemporary vocabulary for description and response.

Leon Battista Alberti's admonition to his Florentine brethren some five hundred years ago is useful for us today. Alberti felt that "it was less difficult for the Ancients" to create great art "because they had models to imitate and from which they could learn." The search for the models of Louisiana painting should be animated and inspired by Alberti's desire that our own "fame ought to be much greater, then, if we discover unheard-of and never-before-seen arts...without any model whatsoever."[4] As we view the lesser-known painting of Louisiana, placing it in the context of national and international movements, we may indeed create that perspective of ideas which will result in a greater appreciation of the art at hand, and the culture from which it came.

ACKNOWLEDGMENTS

FROM THE OUTSET OF this project, initiated by the New Orleans Museum of Art, it became apparent that the most important collections of research materials were not of a primary nature. Artists' letters and documents surviving from the period under consideration are quite rare. It is hoped that this comprehensive survey of the first 150 years of painting in Louisiana may indeed prompt further, deeper research into the subject, with exhibitions and monographs on individual artists and associations to follow in the future.

The notes at the end of the book provide the proper citation for further documentation. However, it is important to acknowledge the resources and assistance that I received from a number of generous individuals and institutions.

The artist files at the Historic New Orleans Collection represent the most substantial body of information available to the student of Louisiana painting. These files provided the source materials for the *Encyclopaedia of New Orleans Artists 1718-1918,* published by the Historic New Orleans Collection in 1987, the foundation of this volume. The HNOC also has important primary and secondary materials relating the 1884 Cotton Exposition, the Arts and Crafts Club, and Josephine Crawford. At the HNOC I am particularly grateful to John A. Mahe II, Judith Bonner, and Joanne P. Platou.

The New Orleans Museum of Art, which mounted the exhibition complemented by this volume, has the entire archives of the WPA Art Project, including the papers of the Woodward brothers, and the research notes for the books on Louisiana painters compiled by the Project. While the entire staff at NOMA was most supportive, I must especially thank those colleagues who worked with me on this project: William Fagaly, Daniel Piersol, Paul Tarver, Carl Penny, Owen Murphy, Tara McNeely, Sharon Litwin, and, especially, the director, E. John Bullard.

The generosity of the Roger Houston Ogden Collection to this project was essential to its success. Not only is the Ogden

Collection the finest grouping of Louisiana paintings in private hands, it also is well documented. Access to curatorial information and color transparencies was made possible by Ken Barnes and Ann Ogden. Deepest appreciation and admiration go to Roger Ogden for his dedication to forming this extraordinary collection.

The Louisiana State Museum is to be congratulated for the primary materials gathered in Scrapbooks 100 and 101. These documents represent this topic's only substantial primary materials of the nineteenth century. Burt Harter, Curator of Painting, was most helpful with research and generously gave me access to the many paintings in storage.

The Louisiana Room at the Howard-Tilton Memorial Library at Tulane University is an important archival resource, particularly in the areas of Newcomb School pottery and materials on a variety of artists. The curator of the Tulane University Art Collection, William R. Cullison III, was most helpful in showing me relevant works. Professor Jessie J. Poesch, of Newcomb College Art Department, the dean of Southern art historians, was a wonderful guide who was very willing to listen.

H. Parrott Bacot, who as director of the Anglo-American Art Museum at the Louisiana State University, Baton Rouge, has assembled an enviable collection of Louisiana art, shared with me his extensive knowledge of private collections and acted as a consultant on attributions. The Baton Rouge Art League's strong collection of Louisiana WPA art has been reinforced by a catalog prepared by Professor Richard Cox.

It remains to acknowledge the help and support of several fine individuals. The collection of William E. Groves, made over a fifty-year period, provided much of the interest in the study of Louisiana painting. Neal Alford, Donald Didier, and Timothy J. Foley, of the Tilden-Foley Gallery, were most helpful in locating paintings for study.

Finally, the spirit of this volume is dedicated to Mr. Raymond Samuel, whose recent death removed a profound figure in Louisiana's cultural history. Mr. Samuel was always personally supportive of my scholarship, acting as a mentor and friend. This dedication is made with scholarly devotion and warm regards for his widow, Martha Ann.

DOWNRIVER

Currents of Style in Louisiana Painting 1800-1950

CHAPTER ONE

Jose de Salazar: Sources and Implications of Colonial Portraiture

As the two main streams of colonial Louisiana culture reflect the lingering strains of the French and Spanish Baroque style, it is only appropriate to begin this study with an exploration of the art of the portrait artist Jose de Mendoza y Salazar. Really very little is known about the artist's life. There is a small body of portraiture extant either known to have been painted by the artist or attributed to him. But even among these a sufficient disparity of style exists to call into question whether there was indeed one artist whom we can identify as "Salazar" or perhaps, more accurately, a similar style derived from several sources and practiced by several painters.

By all accounts, Salazar was born in Merida, Yucatan, Mexico, of a "prominent Creole family."[1] To the Creole mind, "prominent" and "Creole" were redundant for the Creoles "had a certain social standing, if not actual wealth, and definite pretentions to culture and elegance."[2] This may have fostered a taste for portraiture in the Spanish colonial high style.

Precisely when Salazar arrived in New Orleans is uncertain. When George David Coulon gave Bror Wikstrom his notes on "old painters in New Orleans" in 1899, he writes that Salazar was "flourishing about 1769."[3] Coulon's long career in nineteenth-century New Orleans, and his venerable position as the dean of Louisiana painters, makes him a creditable source for folklore, if not for actual documentation.

Coulon observes that Salazar was the "oldest painter I know of" and goes on to record that the artist "assisted by his son...made all the old family portraits in Louisiana. He also painted many small religious pictures and a few large church paintings." Where Coulon's account comes into question is in regard to his dating Salazar's portraits of Don Carlos and Charlotte Trudeau. Not only does Coulon reverse their names in his account, referring to them as the Trudeau Leveauxs, but dates the works 1769. Mrs. Trudeau is not thought to have been born until 1760, and Don Carlos Trudeau, whom Coulon accurately describes as the state surveyor, was not appointed to that position until 1773.

School of Salazar
Mrs. Ignacio de Balderes and Daughter, circa 1790
oil on canvas
46 x 36 5/8 inches
Louisiana State Museum, 141.1

Nevertheless, the suggestion that Salazar was in New Orleans as early as 1769 is worthy of consideration, for in that year, the definitive change of authority, from French rule to Spanish administration, occurred. This shift of ownership of colonial Louisiana from one Bourbon dynasty to the other is more than the mere trade of patents royal. It marks a sea change in the cultural identity of the region.

Louisiana, which had been founded as a French colony by Bienville and which had sustained close ties with French Canada, was by virtually all accounts a disastrous episode in colonial development. Initially populated by the very dregs of French society, the colony had done little to distinguish itself by the time of Spanish rule. No existing artwork survives from that period, whether as the result of a lack of interest, or as the result of the devastating fires which struck New Orleans in 1788 and 1794.

The emergence of Creole culture with the attendant taste for which it was renowned involves several rather complex ironies. Subsequent generations of Creole historians, notably the aristocratic intellectual Charles Gayarré, cherished the notion of a foundering French colony redeemed by authoritarian regimes of Spanish officers in charge, even as they continued to speak French and prize, above all else, the nuances of French culture. "It must be admitted," wrote Gayarré in his nineteenth-century history of Louisiana, "that Louisiana has been, since its foundation...in a starving condition; that being deficient in the knowledge of its internal resources, or rather in energy or will to develop them, it had been almost entirely dependent...on the mother country which could no longer supply its wants...."[4]

The colonial French culture in Louisiana spawned a passionately loyal, highly romantic succession of descendants who wreaked great revenge on the occupying Spanish. Yet there is nothing about that culture to indicate that it had any native strength in the colonial period. As the contemporary historian Joe Gray Taylor has written, "Louisiana never prospered under French rule."[5] As of yet, Louisiana had no staple crop, an extremely high trade deficit, and public officials who were notoriously corrupt. Taylor sees these officials, sent from France, as "largely incompetent, venal and corrupt."

From the onset of the French and Indian Wars in the North American continent in 1754 to the Treaty of Paris in 1763, it was clear that France's power in the new world was declining in the face of superior English military organization and venture capital. Although Spain honored the "Family Compact" and came to the aid of the French against the British, it was to no avail. Ultimately Spain, too, was deprived of various New World holdings, including west Florida.

In part to compensate Spain for that assistance, and undoubtedly in even larger part to be rid of the expense of maintaining Louisiana, Louis XV "ceded by the pure effect of the generosity of his heart" Louisiana to King Charles III.[6] The echo of genteel nineteenth-century historiography deserves to be heard on this exchange. The historian Henry Rightor, writing during the 1890s, felt that this exchange occurred because "the King of France was desirous to give his cousin of Spain a proof of the great interest he took in his welfare, and was touched by the sacrifices made by his Catholic Majesty to bring about peace."[7]

School of Salazar
Ignacio de Balderes, circa 1790
oil on canvas
45 1/2 x 33 1/2 inches
Louisiana State Museum, M141.2

Peace is the last thing that came to Louisiana as a result of the departure of French authority. The French street mobs bitterly resented being transferred, as so much chattel, from the authority of one distant colonial power, from which they were at least descended, to another, far more alien authority, whose language they did not speak, and whose religion was known to be far more constraining.

Spain was rather desultory in taking possession of the colony. Not until 1766 did the Spanish appointed official, Don Antonio de Ulloa, arrive in New Orleans. Ulloa did very little to change things, left the existing Council in charge, and as he was a rather distinguished scholar interested in exploration, set about to make an exacting tour of the colony. Things continued pretty much as they had been until 1768 when a regulation preventing the importation of anything but Spanish wines was issued. According to Taylor, "Louisiana being Louisiana...this was the last straw." As Ulloa had only eighty soldiers in his company, a resistance would prove futile, so on November 16, 1768 he sailed for Havana, and the French colonists were left to congratulate themselves for a successful revolution.

That this was to be short lived should come as no surprise to any student familiar with Spanish colonialism. Indeed, the same power that destroyed all the established traditions of the native populations of Central America acted with far greater kindness to the band of European insurrectionaries in Louisiana. In August of 1769, a large fleet, 2,000 soldiers, and a Spanish commander with the unlikely name of O'Reilly arrived in New Orleans and re-established Spanish rule.

O'Reilly, who had been born in Ireland but went to Spain during the period of Irish Catholic oppression, proved to be not only a lenient master, but also a rather brilliant administrator. It was O'Reilly who organized the area, for ecclesiastical purposes, into parishes, an event which was to have a lasting political effect. Furthermore, under his administration, the form of government was changed, and the Cabildo or presiding City Council was created. While these political developments are not our concern here, it is important to consider that they did create a need for architectural and artistic commissions, some of which Salazar fulfilled.

Salazar's first creditable appearance in the surviving documents of Louisiana history occurs in July of 1789 when Mathias James O'Connor, a local official, mentions the artist in his journals. His citation, "pay Don Josef Salazar the celebrated self taught portrait painter..." is the source of much subsequent confusion.[8] O'Connor's original handwriting was somewhat difficult to read, and during the 1930s, when the Works Progress Administration undertook a survey of New Orleans artists, this name was transcribed as "Latizar."[9] Consequently, several publications since that time have raised the spectre of a portraitist named Latizar who worked in the same style as Salazar. Lack of definitive documentation has only further confused the issue.

Though brief, O'Connor's mention of Salazar contains a critical phrase: "the celebrated self taught portrait painter..." If Salazar was indeed self-taught, as is not unlikely, how did he develop a compositional format to which he could apply his native genius as a technician? Two possibilities exist: he would almost have surely seen other paintings in his native Yucatan, which was rich in church architecture and religious painting, and he may have been exposed to portrait prints from which he could draw poses, and iconographic significance.

The use of portrait prints as a compositional source for portrait poses is now an accepted fact of all studies of the colonial era. "Borrowings of this kind are one of the natural ingredients of colonial portraiture," according to Richard Saunders' account of Copley's use of engravings based on the work of Sir Joshua Reynolds. In the case of Salazar it is not so much a question of whether he used portrait prints as a source, but what sorts of prints, where they came from, and how he used them to result in a clearly identifiable style.

Coulon's critique of Salazar's style leaves little room for rebuttal. "His paintings are harsh, he was not much of a colorist, but *he made good likenesses.*" Coulon's emphasis that Salazar was adept at a good likeness is as much a reflection of nineteenth-century concerns with "truth" in art as it is a proper evaluation of the artist's ability, but the comments on harshness and coloration are worth considering in the context of the painter's work.

Salazar's surviving portraits may be divided into three categories, with one important subcategory. Consider that the artist's work roughly consists of pendant portraits of husband and wife, the subcategory of portraits of mothers with their children, a large group portrait, and several monumental works in the grand manner. These last served not only as likenesses but as propagandistic objects intended to impress a pluralistic population with the advantages of the socio-political status quo.

Within the first group of Salazar's portraits the most obvious of his portrait conventions emerges. Repeatedly, the artist chooses to place his figure inside a tondo, or oval device. While this device does appear in some preceding European painting, it is most frequently used in seventeenth- and eighteenth-century portrait prints.

It would be most interesting to connect the portraiture of Salazar to developments in Central American art, but the actual compositional sources for his portraiture would seem to derive from European prints in the prevailing high style of Britain and the north. Consistently, the artist places the figure inside his well-drawn, defining tondo, a device which seldom appealed to the Spanish colonial painters of the same period. While they did tend to favor the use of cartouches, and symbolic heraldic devices, their portraiture displays an obvious affection for the lingering baroque style, from whose faintly crude echoes comes the stylistic appeal.

Nor does the shading and modelling of Salazar's work have a florid, baroque feel. Coulon criticizes Salazar's coloration because it lacks the highly keyed quality of the mid-nineteenth-century rococo revival which we can equate with Coulon himself. The subtlety of Salazar's work is a harmonious association of skin tones and costume coloration which blend in a quite well realized and really rather sophisticated compositional whole.

As to format, Salazar's work in the grand manner is larger than the standard English and Anglo-American size, the kit-kat of 36 x 28 inches (height by width). However, of the known Salazar works from which we can draw conclusions most are either 36 x 28 or 32 x 26 inches. Combined with the deep placement of the figure to the picture plane, this trait tends to heighten the grandeur, a simple yet suggestive manifestation of the baroque colonial spirit, indeed the only pronounced baroque element in the entire canon of work.

Colonial grandeur and dignity is precisely what the Spanish may have wanted, and considering the extent to which the Louisiana

School of Salazar
Marianne Celeste Dragon, circa 1795
oil on canvas
37 1/4 x 30 1/4 inches
Louisiana State Museum, 5750

territory became prosperous and orderly during their administration, it is certainly what they deserve. The occupants of Salazar's picture plane are not provincials seen in the clumsy manner of an itinerant of little ability. They are rather respectable types painted with a large amount of dash and bravura by a self-trained artist perhaps, but one with considerable native genius as well.

Several small devices in the artist's work support a claim for his rather original ability as a painter and composer. In the portrait of Marie Celeste Dragon, for instance, the well-realized still life on the elaborately detailed table at which she sits is worthy of Zurburan, the Spanish master. The placement of her hands in a delicately parallel position, reaching for the flowers, has the look and feel of highly stylized court portraiture. Though slightly awkward when compared with the still self-conscious gaze of the sitter, it does rival the works of colonial artists creating a sense of the sitter's social ambitions. These are, after all, objects of great value, being created for a clientele who represent the highest echelons of the local establishment.

Salazar's most repeated and alluring compositional device is seen in the way he seats the figures in his double portraits of mothers with their children. In the manner of the Italian painters of the quattrocento and cinquecento, especially Bellini, Salazar has the seated mother, in the fashion of the madonna, hold a piece of fruit, or a flower, out to the child in her lap, who looks at it and grasps after it in a parallel motion to her own hand.

Consider the figural placement in the portrait of Clarice Le Duc and her infant. With her sidelong glance and tilted head in the

Jose de Salazar (born Mexico, mid-1700s-1802)
Clarice Le Duc and Child, 1791
oil on canvas
40 x 36 1/4 inches
Mrs. Harold H. Stream Collection, New Orleans

Italian tradition, she engages the viewer in a complex geometrical relationship. The parallel rendering of the hands and the slight optical illusion of the fruit between them gives a great sense of depth and perspective to the image.

Whether Salazar actually had access to Italian prints of the artists of the Renaissance is unclear. From studies of Peruvian colonial painting it is clear that religious prints distributed by the Jesuits throughout South America often depicted the same pose as propagated by the cult of the sacred heart. In one published study, Paul Lelman has noted that the printing of souvenir and indulgence sheets brought in new subjects.[10] All of this was added to the repertory and stimulated the imagination of the colonial workshop. With the firm entrenchment of the Roman Catholic church in New Orleans, under the able bishopric of Pere Antoine, it does seem likely that Salazar may have had access to a number of indulgence sheets and religious prints through the auspices of the St. Louis Cathedral. It would be interesting to pinpoint his precise sources for each composition.

However, Salazar was not constrained to derivative compositions. In several of his works he demonstrates an original compositional format of considerable skill. The double portraits of the Trudeaus are highly sophisticated, and establish an ingenious understanding of the two-dimensionality of the picture plane.

Both Trudeaus are seated in a relaxed manner at the backgammon table, paired in a pendant pose, each looking out towards the viewer, and turned in a slight contrapposto manner from the picture plane. Though now separated, it is possible to see that the rendering of the gaming table itself is so closely realized in both pictures and matches up so perfectly that this was once a large group portrait of the genial couple at play. Both display graceful gestures—Don Carlos holding the dice cup, and Charlotte delicately holding aloft her own backgammon piece. As pairs of pendant portraits would have enjoyed a greater decorative popularity in the mid-nineteenth century, it can only be supposed that the pair was divided, with the result of the loss of compositional integrity of the work, although the clarity of the likeness is unaltered.

Salazar's largest extant work is the group portrait of the Montegut family thought to have been painted in the final years of the artist's life. Like the Trudeau portrait it too has been altered. According to the catalog of the Louisiana State Museum, the work is "assumed to be composed of two separate canvases, spliced together."[11] This seems less likely than the division of the Trudeau portrait.

From what we have seen of Salazar's work so far, the awkward divisions between the figures here, if they were indeed two separate canvases, would be inconsistent with the rather consistent compositional ability of the artist. Certainly, the figure of the elderly aunt has been applied by another hand to the group of the parents

Jose de Salazar (born Mexico, mid-1700s-1802)
Don Carlos Laveau Trudeau
35 3/4 x 27 1/2 inches
Tulane University Art Collection, Gift of the Children of Mrs. Angela Labatut Puig, New Orleans

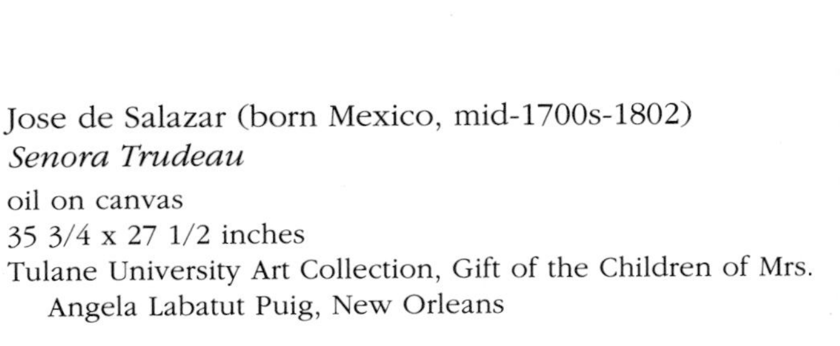

Jose de Salazar (born Mexico, mid-1700s-1802)
Senora Trudeau
oil on canvas
35 3/4 x 27 1/2 inches
Tulane University Art Collection, Gift of the Children of Mrs. Angela Labatut Puig, New Orleans

Jose de Salazar (born Mexico, mid-1700s-1802)
Family of Dr. Joseph Montegut, 1798-1800
oil on canvas
59 x 74 1/2 inches
Louisiana State Museum, 4944-45

on the right of the picture. The portrait of the group of children to the left could also stand alone as a work.

But as a whole the work has a dynamic and group spirit which is unique in the portraiture of colonial Louisiana, indeed rather unique in the canon of all antebellum Louisiana painting. Not until the monumental works of such artists as W. H. Baker and James Henry Wright during the days of the plantation baroque of the 1850s do such ambitious works return. Then again, not until that time would one sitter expend the means to have so large a group painted at one time. Considering that the portrait prices were often derived from the number of likenesses and the anatomical details of each, this was indeed an extensive undertaking.

Salazar's state portraits exemplify his most lasting impact upon the image of Spanish colonial Louisiana. Monumental in scale and rivaling in compositional originality the works of many European painters, they are masterpieces without peer among other colonial painters working in the North American continent at the same time.

On at least two occasions, Salazar painted large-scale, grand-manner portraits for the Louisiana theocracy. Two of these were

Jose de Salazar (born Mexico, mid-1700s-1802)
Clara de la Motte, circa 1795
oil on canvas
30 1/16 x 24 13/16 inches
The Historic New Orleans Collection, 1981.213

Jose de Salazar (born Mexico, mid-1700s-1802)
Mary Minor Kenner, 1802
oil on canvas
37 x 28 inches
City of Kenner Collection, Mayor Aaron F. Broussard

of churchmen, a bishop and a much-loved priest. One was of a local city official whose charitable contributions to the city have left the most lasting architectural statement of the reign.

In the portraits of Bishop Cardenas and Don Andres Almonester y Roxas, Salazar reverts to the far older tradition of using heraldic devices and cartouches with written words right on the surface of the painting. Though a frequent device in the Spanish visual tradition of the seventeenth century, this technique and visual presentation enjoyed no currency whatsoever in the world of the late eighteenth century, and is a most curious throwback.

Both Cardenas and Roxas were responsible for helping to transform the chaos of the Louisiana territory into a prosperous state. Their presentation in so recherche a fashion may in part be a tribute to the stability and harmony of an existing social order, far older than the recent developments in Louisiana. Presenting them in the grand manner is a direct tribute to their personal successes.

The portrait of Roxas was commissioned by the Cabildo in recognition of the generosity of that gentleman towards the city in several times of need. The minutes of the Cabildo record the intention of the commission and the possible source for the cartouche and its legend:

> As it seems to the commissioners that the city is anxious to express to the said benefactor how grateful we are, in an honourable and creditable manner for said buildings, which is the only thing his modesty would accept, the commissioners agreed that with city funds, a portrait of the said Don Andres be made and placed in the chambers of the Cabildo, with the proper inscription concerning his deeds of liberality.[12]

Don Andres was a crown official, and his heraldic shield on the lower left of the painting bears tribute to his rank in the community. Roxas's generosity may have been an atonement for his accumulated wealth, much of it attained in a spirit of what would now be known as insider trading, as he enjoyed a particularly favored treatment by the Cabildo.

Through his patronage the Cabildo, the Presbytere, and the St. Louis Cathedral were built. These buildings replaced the earlier structures, which were destroyed in the disastrous fire of 1788. It had levelled much of the older French settlement, leading to the extensive rebuilding program of the late eighteenth century and resulting in the arrangement of the Vieux Carré as it may be seen today.

As these works in so vast a scale would have been very demanding, it seems likely that Salazar was assisted in their composition by his daughter, Francesca. It is known that she made a copy on her own of the portrait of Bishop Cardenas, and perhaps

Jose de Salazar (born Mexico, mid-1700s-1802)
Bishop Penalver y Cardenas, 1802
oil on canvas
85 x 52 inches
Louisiana State Museum, 1955.8

Jose de Salazar (born Mexico, mid-1700s-1802)
Don Andres Almonester y Roxas, 1796
oil on canvas
72 x 48 inches
The Roman Catholic Church of the Archdiocese of New Orleans

she functioned as a background painter in the tradition of European masters, like Rubens, who had assistants.

Salazar did not live to see the next steps of changes in the cultural image of Louisiana. What he achieved can be measured in very precise terms. Salazar was the first painter of note to work in the region, and created a body of portraiture of considerable sophistication and visual clarity. The mere fact that he was able to work on a grand scale in his more important state commissions separates him from the usual colonial portrait artists. He was also responsible for creating an image of the Spanish colonial ascendancy that is as enduring in the visual arts as the buildings of Almonester are in the world of three dimensions.

His legacy as an artist is far more difficult to ascertain. It is still unclear whether the works which are attributed to him were indeed the work of his hand, or in his style. Some are signed but many others are not. Works attributed to Salazar have been done so on the basis of certain compositional similarities and the repetition of certain devices, such as the tondo, or porthole. The thinly painted and delicately colored works may have influenced other artists in the area of which we have no record.

Unlike the painters of the colonial northeast, whose style was imitated and which evolved through several successive generations in the antebellum period, Salazar had no precedent and no readily identifiable followers. The portrait styles of Louisiana change substantially in the years following his death.

The great population shift in the region follows the American purchase, the Battle of New Orleans, and the invention of the steamboat. The flooding of the territory with Americans created a determined and persistent affinity for the emerging American style of Federal neoclassicism. The artists who brought that style south were far more adventurous and less settled than Salazar, and their sitters offer the next surging current in this history.

CHAPTER TWO

The French and American Schools in New Orleans

SALAZAR'S DEATH IN 1803 came at a time when the uneasy cultural assimilation between the French and Spanish cultures was being eroded by the emerging American nation. Although their migration was technically illegal, hundreds of English-speaking frontiersmen had already found their way downriver to New Orleans. Their legendary raucous behavior, subsequently encased in a lively, enduring folklore, led to the rise of an image of New Orleans as a rowdy terminus on the principal continental pathway.

The American Revolution, which secured a free state for the Eastern and Southern colonies, culminated in a political entity representing a rather formidable challenge to the ambitions of Napoleon Bonaparte. Louisiana, meanwhile, had been traded, yet again, from Spain, who had not wanted the left luggage of the Bourbon dynasts in the first place. Once again, the erstwhile French-speaking territory was in the hands of France. Napoleon's ambitions knew few bounds, and the little corporal of the first empire saw in Louisiana possibilities for restoring French prestige, and wealth, in the new world.

However symbolic, Napoleon's repatriation of Louisiana to the mother country was greeted with swells of enthusiasm by those Louisiana natives who continued to see themselves as a part of the larger French culture. Although the Spanish had provided the French Louisianans with something the French themselves had never been able to grant—prosperity—the local population still felt a deep ethnic bond with France.

Prosperity added a glaze of respectability to previous generations. It was at this time that the strong cultural undercurrent of high Creole culture began to emerge. To quote George Washington Cable, it was a "quiet narrow way which a lover of Creole antiquity, in fondness for a romantic past," followed to the high noon of antebellum life. Interwoven into the plastic arts of the period, especially in architecture and portraiture, is a healthy exchange between the nostalgic longings of the Creoles for things French and the spirit of the young Americans who surged into their midst upon the very tide of the great river at hand.

Confrontation with the Americans was inevitable. Napoleon's dreams, in most arenas, proved futile, especially his dreams for the Louisiana territory far removed from his shaky continental empire. Swamped by British sea power, and pressed in Europe, he agreed to enter negotiations with the government of President Thomas Jefferson to consummate a Louisiana purchase agreement. Ultimately commissioners Robert Livingston and James Monroe paid the French some fifteen million dollars for the land mass which more than doubled the size of the fledgling United States and changed, forever, the demographic composition and cultural terrain of Louisiana.

Writing of the Louisiana Purchase in his classic *History of the United States of America During the Administrations of Jefferson & Madison,* Henry Adams describes the "annexation...[as] an event so portentous as to defy measurement; it gave a new face to politics, and ranked in historical importance next to the Declaration of Independence and the adoption of the Constitution...." The purchase was the first test of the emerging American melting pot theory, for the vast majority of the young nation was English-speaking and of English descent. Now they faced a new cultural imperative, peoples whom, in the words of Adams, "were unfit for self-government, and must be treated as a conquered race until they learned to consider themselves American citizens."[1]

While all of this political turmoil and social change may have been good for the homogenization of Louisiana culture, it did not immediately create a new climate of taste for portraiture. It seems worth speculating that various works still extant which bear the Salazar attribution were really painted at this time by imitators of that artist who continued to work in his style late into the first decade of the nineteenth century. Overall, if we are to judge by the lack of existing examples, portrait activity was at a minimum.

Of all the plastic arts, portraiture is the one manifestation most specifically linked to developments in the local economy and to those trends in popular imagination which we call style. Any portrait may be analyzed by a simple formula calibrating the artist's ability and the subject's ambitions, for a portrait is almost always the result of ways and means...the ways of the artist, and the means of the sitter.

For those very reasons, the study of portraiture is almost inevitably linked to social history, largely because the images of individuals which survive from the past become our only means of "seeing" those times, or at least those who inhabited them. Criticism of the study of portraiture as an investigation of the elite aspects of the overall society is not altogether deserved. Portrait artists of varying talents, charging a wide variety of prices, functioned in the Louisiana territory, and not all the images which survive are of a ruling elite painted in the grand manner.

Those which do survive indicate the extent to which the sitter showed some awareness of prevailing artistic trends. The paucity of portrait artists working in New Orleans quickly gave way as the territory opened and large numbers of artists flocked to the newly wealthy city to seek their fortunes. Once there, they became the agents for transforming artistic consensus. "From the very beginning," writes Barbara Novak, "artists in America have tried to create measurable certainties...."[2] Little in life is as certain as an anxious, demanding sitter, posed before the brush of the portrait painter.

At the very moment the American government was attempting to instruct the citizens of the new Louisiana territory on the virtues, and advantages, of citizenship, young American portrait artists were finding their way to New Orleans. Amongst the first of whom there is any mention is the Kentucky painter William Edward West.[3] According to family tradition West may have made his first trip to New Orleans as early as 1803 near the time of the transfer of power from France to the United States. At that time he is thought to have been travelling in the company of a hemp and tobacco merchant, and almost certainly stopped in Natchez, where there were strong Kentucky connections.

West is mentioned at that time as being a miniaturist, an art for which there was considerable demand, for fashion and for portability into turbulent frontier territories. One of the West miniatures which survives is of the very Abram Spears, tobacco merchant, with whom West is thought to have made the Southern journey.

West's subsequent place in the history of art in Louisiana has been secured by the questionable attribution of a supposed painting of the battle of New Orleans said to have been executed in 1815. Similarities between the rather well known print *Battle of New Orleans and Death of Major General Pakenham on the 8th of January 1815*, engraved by J. Yeager in 1817 and printed in Philadelphia, and Benjamin West's painting of *The Death of General Wolfe* only add to the confusion. William Edward West was often mistaken for the far better known Benjamin West, president of the Royal Academy, an association of names he was reluctant to deny.

Whatever the threads of the painting's attribution, they do coincide with certain important developments in the life of West as an artist. At various times between 1812 and 1817 he had been in Philadelphia studying, or perhaps more accurately, painting with the great romantic master Thomas Sully. West absorbed much of Sully's technique in those years, and together with far more well known portraitists such as John Vanderlyn and John Wesley Jarvis, helped to introduce the American neoclassical style into the Deep South.

The entrance of American neoclassical portraiture into the canon of Louisiana artistic style does indeed mark a visual departure from that small body of portraiture we have seen so far. Salazar, though talented and innovative, was practicing a particularly idiosyncratic technique. With their faint echoes of European high style, which has an element of caricature, his portraits are from a fascinating, though provincial, hand.

With the advent of West and the subsequent legions of American artists who poured into the city following the opening of the river to steamboat trade in 1815, the most obvious symbol of assimilation into American culture was the adoption of the neoclassic portrait style. As a portrait style, neoclassicism, as practised by the Americans, both itinerant and resident, was at once expedient and sophisticated. As perfected by Gilbert Stuart and Thomas Sully, it depicted the subject with minimal anatomical detail, especially in those works which display only the head and shoulders, while focusing with some deftness upon the character as well as the likeness of the sitter.

Despite several rather well worn and erroneous folk stories, itinerant artists did not go about with canvases of painted bodies to which they added heads as the commission arose. That theory may be disproved by a formal analysis of the neoclassical portrait formula. The artist practices the traditional method of creating a space for the likeness upon the picture plane by halving the canvas vertically, with a line drawn from top to bottom. When this division is repeated by a line drawn across the center horizon line, an *l* bracket is formed by the perpendicular intersection. The likeness is then "hung" within this *l* bracket. Indeed, the entire process of the portrait begins by sketching in the facial features and working out from the center of the picture plane to the other anatomical features and background details. Most sitters did not care to sit for long periods and usually left the studio once the face had been painted, leaving the portrait artist, or his assistant, to complete the work.

Many portrait painters made their reputations as much by their ability to entertain their subjects during the tedious posing period as by their actual craft. West was a well-known raconteur, as was his contemporary and fellow Kentuckian Matthew Harris Jouett. (Indeed, in considering Jouett's merits as a portraitist the quaint early American art historian William Dunlap remarked that "his astonishing powers of conversation and companionable disposition, caused his society to be constantly courted, and gave him an amount of employment never enjoyed by any other artist in the west."[4]) Craft, conversation, and a willingness to travel were clearly the itinerant's stock in trade.

West's frequent trips south during the decade 1810-20 represent one pattern of itinerant portrait activity followed by many of the artists during this time of the opening of the Louisiana territory to American culture. The appearance in New Orleans of several well-known American artists gives an insight into the typological routes followed by successive generations.

Itinerancy was really of two types. First, there were those artists who appeared, at irregular intervals, in Louisiana during the warm winter months, seeking commissions from the locals. It seems to have been a lucrative situation, for as one of Audubon's editors has remarked, "it was not primarily an intellectual society but rather a social one, where the opera was the best supported of the arts, with family portraiture a second."[5] From such accomplished artists as John Vanderlyn and John Wesley Jarvis, the list of seasonal itinerants dwindles down through the precious few known minor artists, such as Edmund Brewster and C. R. Parker, to the legions of unknown artists who have left behind a large body of unidentifiable work which represents most of the canon of early nineteenth-century portraiture in the South.

Far more important is the second type of itinerant who can be seen in Louisiana, the resident itinerant. Many portraitists who came to Louisiana in the antebellum period either stayed for extended visits or took up permanent residency. Of these, Theodore Sidney Moise, W. H. Baker, and Robert Gschwindt are examples. Once the French painters began to paint in New Orleans during the 1830s, an international itinerancy began to have a substantial impact upon taste in the city.

West's impact was far more lengthy than his tenure. Apart from one portrait he rendered of Julien de Poydras, who presided over the first state constitutional convention in 1817, little else is known of his work in Louisiana, although numerous examples of his work in the Natchez region during the same period are extant. Following his stay in New Orleans, West departed for Europe, where he painted the last life portrait of Lord Byron. This event created an enduring aura of success about a local itinerant who achieved fame on the international scale.

West's successes were really the inspiration for the travels of Matthew Harris Jouett and Joseph Henry Bush, his fellow Kentuckians, as well as Chester Harding and James Reid Lambdin. Harding and Lambdin were Northern itinerants who had worked, and studied, in the central Kentucky region, bringing their skills to the traditions of that region. As the Kentucky portrait market

William Edward West (1788-1857)
Portrait of Julien de Lallande Poydras, 1817
oil on canvas
35 x 28 inches
Poydras Home, New Orleans

played out during the winter months, they too sought the downriver path to prosperity. However, their appearance in New Orleans occurred after West's departure for Europe in 1819. Up until that point, very few portraitists of note appear in the newspaper accounts or advertisements.

The paucity of portraitists in the city had not gone unnoticed by the more informed of the citizenry...especially those desiring to have their likenesses taken. "Within two or three years," one commentator to the Louisiana *Gazette* for April 10, 1819 observed, "we have had persons among us styling themselves 'Portrait Painters', but except in a few instances, their painting required a label on them to enable even a friend to suspect for whom they were designed."

One of the artists who did appear in New Orleans between 1815 and 1820 created a stir by the remarkable number of copies he made, and profitably placed, of the great men of the day. Edmund Brewster, who inspired the above remarks, was an artist from Philadelphia, with the same affection for Stuart and Sully as held by West. As evidence of this devotion, he copied and exhibited Stuart's Landsdowne Washington, and became embroiled in a controversy over whether he had indeed copied a religious genre painting by Sully.

Brewster exhibited his Washington portrait at Maspero's coffeehouse, a sufficiently public exposure to guarantee him the attention he needed to attract portrait commissions. He then advertised his presence in the local papers, in much the same manner as all the artists in the antebellum period, announcing that he "pledges himself to use every exertion to satisfy those who shall encourage him; and unless he produces an approved likeness no charge will be made."[6] The same admirer who remarked upon the excellence of the Stuart copy by Brewster had high hopes for the Yankee itinerant. "I sincerely hope the artist may meet with such encouragement as to be induced to remain with us, till he retrieves the character of several of his brother artists from that disgrace their drawings so justly merited."[7]

Brewster has left few works behind, the most important being a full-length portrait of Father Antonio de Sedella (1748-1829), affectionately known as Pere Antoine, painted in 1822 for the priest's parish church, now St. Louis Cathedral. This portrait, inspired in part by Brewster's knowledge of Stuart's work, was probably intended to complement the earlier Salazar full-length portraits of Bishop Cardenas and Don Andres Almonester. Brewster's portrait is less stiff and formal than Salazar's. He has placed Pere Antoine in an architectonic device that employs a traditional vanishing perspective. The priest is seen in the unworldly guise of a monk—bearded, his head is shaven in a tonsure, and he is shod in sandals. He stands in a hesitant and self-effacing manner next to an open

Joseph Henry Bush
General Zachary Taylor, 1848
oil on canvas
60 x 48 inches
Louisiana State Museum

Edmund Brewster (born circa 1784-94, active New Orleans, 1819-24)
Pere Antoine (Father Antonio de Sedella), 1822
oil on canvas
72 x 46 inches
The Roman Catholic Church of the Archdiocese of New Orleans

Edmund Brewster (born circa 1784-94, active New Orleans, 1819-24)
Portrait of Mr. John Beebe, 1819
oil on panel
10 x 7 7/8 inches
New Orleans Museum of Art, Gift of Muriel Bultman Francis, 71.20

book, either a missal or the Bible itself. The empty unadorned chair on his left is a subtle symbol of the position in which he serves. It is not a bishop's seat, but a chair of the type found in a European cathedral chapter house, representing Sedella's role as a member of the bishop's administrative council.

Among other works remaining from Brewster's years in New Orleans is a portrait of Mr. John Beebe. As it has a pinched and rather frightening quality, totally devoid of the rounded line and benign gaze of his more accomplished neoclassical works, such as his Pere Antoine portrait, it cannot be imagined that Brewster found an altogether warm reception.

Brewster's potential disappointments, and the reviewer's lament about the inappropriate nature of some portrait likenesses, is a concern which the artist John James Audubon well understood. Though Audubon is far better known for his ornithological works, his series of famous engravings, and his books, he did become an itinerant portraitist during his years in Louisiana, 1821-26. Not always successful, he did, nevertheless, leave behind a wonderfully detailed and frank journal recording his experiences. It gives us a rare insight into the life of an itinerant, as well as commentary upon the presence of other well-known artists of the day.[8]

Among the first of those individuals whom Audubon encountered was the New York painter, John Wesley Jarvis. Jarvis seems to have made his first appearance in New Orleans during the 1810s, with the young apprentice Henry Inman as his assistant.[9] They were there in the winter of 1820-21, a period which has been noted as very financially profitable to Jarvis. According to one account, Jarvis "had an abundance of sitters, receiving six a day..." with Inman painting "background and draperies under his teacher's direction."[10]

Jarvis's presence in New Orleans may be documented by a citation in Audubon's journal of his trip to the city in 1821. Audubon had arrived in New Orleans on January 6, 1821, following a lengthy trip downriver by flatboat. He arrived in the city with very little money. Driven by his determination to create a record of the birds of North America, he set about to support himself by his "pencil," as portraitists in those days spoke of their brush. Audubon's determination has the familiar ring of nineteenth-century melodrama as he vows that "my talents are to be my support and my enthusiasm my guide in difficulties, the whole of which I am ready to keep and to surmount."

In keeping with the observation about interest in the arts being restricted to theatres and families, one of Audubon's first encounters was with an Italian artist from the opera company. He took Audubon back to the theatre where the fledgling ornithological illustrator was "very roughly offered...$100 per month to paint...." Audubon, self-confident if not self-secure, protested that "I believe really now that my talents must be poor to the country."

Feeling entirely dejected, Audubon visited the studio of Jarvis, and attempted to convince that artist to allow him to paint in the background details: "Asked him if he needed assistance to finish his portraits i. e. the clothing and grounds—he stared." This is at the time when it had been thought that Henry Inman was in the company of Jarvis, performing those very studio functions for which Audubon pleaded that he "would not turn my back to anyone for such employment and that I had received good lessons from good masters." Jarvis merely put Audubon off.

Written evidence of an interest in painting background details is yet more proof of the headless body myth. Audubon's offer of help is a clear indication that the portrait artist worked out from the head, then filling out slowly, and in accord with the price set for background and clothing details. Throughout this period the standard price for a head and shoulder portrait was $50. Additional anatomical details, such as hands, or specific background details such as a vase of flowers or a bit of landscape glimpsed through the drapery, would likely cost the sitter an additional sum. Half-length portraits and full-length works cost in the range of $100 to $250.

Jarvis did not reject Audubon outright, but rather summoned him back to his painting rooms the next day. There, "he asked me many questions until" Audubon "thought that he feared my assistance." This was not to be, for Jarvis told Audubon that "he could not believe that I could help him in the least." Thus ended the encounter in New Orleans between two of the young nation's best-known artists.

Although few survive, Audubon did render, as his journal indicates, several likenesses with his pencil. These seem to have been of the pastel variety, for which Audubon notes that he charged twenty-five dollars. The supplies which he would have needed, not to mention a stable space in which to create oil portraits, were beyond the artist's resources. Taking these likenesses were, after all, but a means to an end for Audubon and the numbers of portraits subsequently attributed to him are more likely by a man of renown than this struggling painter with limited funds.

Never one to hide his feelings, certainly not in his journal, Audubon is able to note, on at least one occasion, the unpleasant experience of having a work rejected. "I met this morning with one of those slight discouraging incidents connected with the life of the artists; I had a likeness spoken of in very rude terms by the fair lady it was made for, and perhaps will lose my time and the reward expected for my labor."

Audubon had one other encounter with an American artist of note while he was in New Orleans. Seeking to obtain yet another letter of recommendation for his ornithological project, Audubon called upon an eminent "historical painter" with his portfolio. Although John Vanderlyn professed no knowledge of bird life, or Audubon's ability to render it accurately, he agreed to write the letter, which prompted Audubon to question in his journal if "all men of talents are fools and rude purposely or naturally?"[11] It seems to be a sad demise for Vanderlyn, one of the most celebrated painters of his day, to meet, on his way down, one who would soon be one of the first overnight success stories of American art.

Even as Audubon was sketching in the French Quarter and foraging in the market for bird specimens to draw, the itinerants from Kentucky continued to flock to New Orleans. They established winter studios and created works which mirrored an ongoing affection for the spare, sophisticated manner of Stuart and Sully. Of these Matthew Harris Jouett made the most lasting impression.

As mentioned, Jouett had a very engaging personality, and was a very excellent portraitist. His surviving letters and reminiscences give an indication of his range of interest, as well as critical insights upon technique. In the literature of the Colonial Revival period he is most often remembered and praised for having been Stuart's favorite "pupil," largely because of an extended visit between the two painters in Boston.[12] Jouett kept a detailed journal of this visit, a chronicle which accounts for the most substantial knowledge we have of the techniques of any itinerant painter of the period.

Jouett actually made a sketch of the way Stuart laid out his palette, as well as taking notes on Stuart's observations about the proper means of taking a likeness. Stuart's modified perception of late-eighteenth-century notions of the sublime and the beautiful in nature and art led him to advise the young portraitist to imitate life, and not art, in the creative process. "To produce a good effect you must copy nature..." Stuart advised Jouett.[13]

Stuart's further admonition seems to have been the one which Jouett took most to heart, for "too much light destroys as too little hides the colors, and that the true and perfect image of man is to be seen only in a misty or hazy atmosphere." Jouett's portraits often have the same watery, shimmering quality as the works of Stuart's late period, when the old master was really in his most innovative phase.

Devotion to Stuart's technique and aesthetic make Jouett's works relatively easy to identify. It was a style apparently discussed amongst the entire central Kentucky school, for many of their works have a marked similarity of coloration, atmospherics, and placement of the figure on the picture plane. A previously unidentified work in the Louisiana State Museum collection has many of those characteristics. The pale and rather muddy background is offset by the fresh and highly colored face. That the costume seems to have a sense of motion is not surprising. Jouett's greatest belief, and the strongest feature of his work, is his mastery of the technique of applying a heightened white finish to the surface of his works. By mixing spirits of turpentine into the white paint of his palette, Jouett achieved a rather lively effect which offsets the characterization of the facial features. "It assists to evaporate the oil & leaves the white a standing white & free from the yellowness occasioned by the oil," Jouett quotes Stuart as observing.

Matthew Harris Jouett
Portrait of a Woman, circa 1840
oil on canvas
30 x 25 inches
Louisiana State Museum, T2.1966

Jouett's letters and the remarks attributed to him are free from the pious intentions of Audubon, devoid of the driven nature of the poor struggling artist personality which Audubon so self-consciously sought to typify. His devotion to Stuart, and his admiration for Sully are slavish, though not without a whimsical touch to be expected from a backwoodsman. He once wrote to Sully that "all the young gentlemen of the brush in this country look upon you as the Elijah of the arts, and push forward with hopes of immortality if they can but touch the hem of your cloak—and so you see if you are annoyed by we poor children of the brush, you must attribute it mainly to that good report which accompanies your name."

While in New Orleans, Jouett frequently met with Jarvis. They could often be seen sitting together, according to one contemporary account, "at the Cafe del Aguilas, at the corner of St. Ann and Chartres Streets, playing dominoes together, or engaged, likely enough, in hot argument with regard to the merit of Gilbert Stuart...."[14] Jouett's devotions were consistent, though his trips to Louisiana were perhaps less profitable than he might have liked.

Writing to Sully in 1822, he remarks that "I visited Louisiana last winter and spring but done but little. I intent another visit this winter hoping for a more fruitful harvest."[15] He was to continue his seasonal visits until 1827, when a sudden illness resulted in his death at the relatively early age of thirty-eight.

The variety of artists with abilities ranging from highly refined to virtually nonexistent says more about the myth of prosperity and opportunity in the new state than it really does about the demand for portraiture. Leaving the decade of the 1820s, one has the sense that the spare American style of portraiture had been imposed, rather like the new form of government, upon a population which still longed for a far more stylish and mature culture. Works like those of Chester Harding and Charles Colson display a more intricate compositional format, far more related to genre painting than to simple profile portraiture.

At the same time, the arrival of portrait artists like C. R. Parker, an enormously prolific painter, gives some indication of market demand for portraiture in a period when the river trade pushed the port of New Orleans into a premier national position. Parker first appears in Louisiana in 1825 when he completed a commission to copy portraits of Washington and Lafayette for the Louisiana state house. These were greatly admired by the New Orleans *Argus* of December 2, 1826, as the "execution does credit to the genius and skill of the artist." Parker is known to have exhibited with the Free Society of Artists in London (1828-29), and at the Royal Academy. Audubon was in England by that time, gaining ground to have his

Attributed to C. R. Parker (active New Orleans, 1826-48)
Mrs. Thomas Beck, circa 1835
38 x 36 inches
Louisiana State Museum, 12039.2

Charles Colson (active New Orleans, 1837)
Portrait of a Creole Lady, 1837
oil on canvas
32 x 25 1/2 inches
Louisiana State Museum, 5792

drawings converted into a series of prints, and he is reputed to have sat for Parker.

Back in New Orleans in 1832, Parker opened a studio on Canal Street and was subsequently in and out of New Orleans with seasonal regularity between 1832 and 1848. His work was greatly admired at the time, as expressed in the New Orleans *Bee* for December 2, 1847: "The characteristics of Mr. Parker's portraits are boldness and fidelity, accuracy of expression, warmth of coloring and exquisite distribution of light and shade." One final mention of him occurs in January of 1848, after which he disappears in Italy.

While Parker's work is rather admirably colored, and has a lively, almost folklike quality of expression, there is a tendency to repeat the same composition rather endlessly. Ladies are almost always posed with one arm raised or curving around a chair, and the body blocked in such a way as to suggest that the shoulders are spanning the width of the picture plane. This sameness had induced many people to see Parker as the prime candidate for the headless body theory of itinerant portraiture. He is not really a primitive artist, for there are elements of the English high style in his work, especially the crisp details in the eyes and costumes of his female subjects. As many examples of his art have been discovered, and documented, his is one more itinerant career upon a canvas by now awash with artists.

It was into this setting of American itinerant portrait art, and renewed economic prosperity, that the French painters of the 1830s would make their entrance. They arrived like heralds of the Creole high noon, leaving in their wake one of the most accomplished bodies of portraiture in the history of Southern painting. The first of the important and influential French portrait artists who arrived in New Orleans was Louis Antoine Collas.

By all accounts, Collas led a truly itinerant existence. He is known to have been at the court of the czars in Russia during the turbulent years of the Napoleonic wars, 1803-11, after which he returned to Paris. His first appearance in this country was in Philadelphia in 1816. Later in that year he visited Charleston, South Carolina, where he returned in 1817-18.

Collas's two most extensively documented trips to New Orleans occurred between 1822-24 and 1826-29, after which he is thought to have returned to Paris. As a portraitist he does not show the degree of finished and innovative design that is to be seen in Vaudechamp and Amans. Indeed much of Collas's portraiture has the look and feel of American neoclassical art, as it was being practiced in both Philadelphia and Charleston during the period.

As in his American contemporaries, one may sense a certain affinity for the portrait style of Thomas Sully and the emerging spirit of American romantic art. Throughout the 1820s, Collas would have been competing for both attention and commissions with the strong infatuations of an American public accustomed to the emerging Jacksonian spirit. Thus his portraiture may reflect a keen desire to suit his audience, blending prevailing European techniques with an American compositional format.

Collas's presence in Philadelphia during the late 1810s would have made him familiar with the French community in that city. Sully's portraits of Jean and Mary Sicard David are not only the

Louis Antoine Collas (born France, 1775-1856)
Portrait of a Free Woman of Color, 1829
oil on canvas
38 3/4 x 31 inches
New Orleans Museum of Art, Gift of Felix H. Kuntz, 49.2

prototypical examples of his romantic empire style, but also demonstrate that artist's ability to relate certain French interests to the French and American taste for spareness.

Sully's compositional format in the portrait of Mary David reflects a popular culture vision of ultimate female beauty. Atop a diminutive body, a long neck stretches up to a head drawn in the long, languid elliptical line which will prevail in Southern portraiture until the outbreak of the Civil War in 1861. William Edward West often copied this particular pose during his years in the Deep South.

For depth and perspective and to heighten the modelling and shading of the figure, one very long and strong line is drawn from the top of the costume to the base of the face with a peculiar humplike effect that gives a curiously uneven result. This is to be seen in Collas's portrait of Madame Armant.

Though competent and reflective of substantial portrait trends, the work of Collas cannot be said to have had the significant artistic impact that was achieved by the next round of French painters, Jean Joseph Vaudechamp and Jacques Amans. Vaudechamp makes his first appearance in New Orleans not long after Collas had made his last in 1829. The coincidence of both events and the close ties of the French community in New Orleans and Paris could lead to some general conclusions about the old world's growing interest in the new. Much as the American portrait painters in the same period were being drawn to New Orleans by the possibility of lucrative commissions, word of some citizens' French interests may have attracted a variety of international artists to the city. Many families, like that of Bernard Duchamps, for example, kept in close touch with French relatives, and brought back from visits to France portraits by French artists of great skill and note. These may have helped to create an appetite amongst the dwindling, though very prosperous, French community for portraits created by French artists in a French high style.

Though competently schooled, Vaudechamp enjoyed little reputation in his own country. He studied, in Paris, with Anne-Louis Girodet, who had herself been a student of Jacques Louis David. This generational association with the studio techniques of the great master of French neoclassical art is important when considering the portraits Vaudechamp painted in Louisiana. In true French style, they are highly finished, with a profound degree of facial modelling, a deep glazing, and a minute attention to costume detail.

Vaudechamp has long been considered the master of the Creole portrait. His clientele represent the creme de la creme of the Creole world of business, finance, public service, and plantation ownership.[16] Only rarely did he receive commissions outside this ascendancy. It is to his brush that we can assign those gazes which have defined the look of one aspect of the old French culture, standing at the edge of the economic changes of the Louisiana

Purchase and gazing towards the collapse brought on by the Civil War.

Inevitably, Vaudechamp's portraits, though often intended to be pendants, follow a compositional format laid out for each gender, independent of each other. Male subjects are placed slightly higher on the picture plane, often appearing slightly formal and distant, with a look of controlled authority in their eyes. The portrait of the young Charles Cole Claiborne, for example, has the dignity one might associate with an important member of the American community whose mother was a Creole.

Vaudechamp has several readily identifiable conventions which he uses to depict the figure. His most distinguishing trait is the slight turning of the figure away from the picture plane, in a subtle and rather evocative contrapposto. This adds not only a great depth to single portraits, but when used in pendant pairs of married couples, which would have almost certainly been hung adjacent, gives a great inter-related geometrical quality. It enhances the visual relationship between the works, affirming their interdependence, while drawing the viewer into a compact triangular viewing relationship.

The full impact of Vaudechamp's superb grasp of coloration, design, and his own interpretation of the contrapposto pose is truly evident in his portrait of Antoine Jacques Philippe de Marigny de Mandeville, painted in 1833. Though born in Louisiana, Mandeville had been granted an appointment to the prestigious St. Cyr military academy in France through the courtesies owed his father by the French King Louis Philippe. He remained in France until 1833, when he returned to Louisiana and became an officer in the Orleans Lancers of the Louisiana militia. Such military organizations were prevalent throughout the South and regiments frequently vied with each other for the most colorful uniforms. Mandeville is seen here in a uniform which combines certain French tasseled affectations with the American eagle and tunic. The combination of a dazzling military uniform with the serene and handsome gaze of the sitter renders this one of the premier military portraits painted in the South before the war.

Far more variety exists in Vaudechamp's single portraits of women. In one format they pose wearing large lacy caps or bonnets which often extend nearly to the top of the picture plane. This adds the same degree of visual energy that Jouett found so appealing, though in this instance far more developed and pronounced in the costume's exaggeration. Lingering aspects of chaste neoclassicism are to be found in some works, such as elongated necks and elliptical faces.

In his portraits of women, Vaudechamp was a master at suggesting the subtleties of their personalities, and perhaps, by implication, the very essence of the culture in which they lived. Madame Caliste Villere, daughter-in-law of Governor Villere, a Creole

Jean Joseph Vaudechamp (born France, 1790-1866)
Antoine Jacques Philippe de Marigny de Mandeville, 1833
oil on canvas
46 x 35 inches
Louisiana State Museum, Gift of the Friends of the Cabildo, 1967.1

idol, wrote a short epistle containing "Advice To Her Children" which is a very revealing confessional on the attitudes of the caste Vaudechamp so brilliantly captured. Speaking of the Creole men, she acknowledges that "all…have the fault of being quick tempered and foul mouthed; they do not sufficiently understand the…sensitivity of women." This coarseness, she writes, "comes from early training, they are not taught self control…." Speaking for her own gender, Madame Villere asserts that "we have a tender nature and are delicate, we feel keenly the need to be treated with consideration."[17]

A far more probing sensitivity attends Vaudechamp's portraits of his female subjects. They peer out from the picture plane with a look that combines a vulnerable awareness with a slightly sharp and defensive gaze. He is often most successful in his portraits of older female subjects, as we may see in the case of Mrs. Theodore Bailly-Blanchard, who purses her lips together over her toothless gums and holds her eyeglasses aloft as commandingly as though she grasped a scepter.

Vaudechamp's tenure extends intermittently throughout the 1830s, during which time he frequently kept a studio on Royal Street in a block now occupied by the famous restaurant The Court of Two Sisters. The time he passed in Louisiana must have been profitable, for Dunlap notes that Vaudechamp made $30,000 during three winters' stay in New Orleans between 1831 and 1834.[18] The artist is thought to have crossed the Atlantic every fall, arriving in New Orleans in November and remaining until late April or early May. Apparently he made enough from these ventures to retire from the field, for after 1839 there is little mention of him in the city again, and he died in France in 1866.

Jean Joseph Vaudechamp (born France, 1790-1866)
Mrs. Theodore Bailly-Blanchard, 1832
oil on canvas
32 x 25 1/2 inches
Louisiana State Museum, 1982.45.1

Whether intentionally or merely by association, Vaudechamp passed his place in the French community of New Orleans along to Jacques Amans, another French portrait artist who arrived in the city in the late 1830s. Vaudechamp and Amans are known to have exhibited in the same salons in Paris and to have travelled to New Orleans on the same boats, so the association was not one of coincidence.

Amans' position in the community of Louisiana was far more integral than that of a seasonal itinerant. He became a landowner with the purchase of the sugar plantation Trinity on the Bayou Lafourche and he married a woman from New Orleans, Azoline Landreaux, in 1844. Amans was actively involved with the affairs of his plantation until the immediate antebellum period, when he and his wife returned to France. He remained there for the rest of his life.

Amans adapted, and used to great effect, many of the same compositional devices which Vaudechamp introduced into Louisiana portraiture. There is the same slight turning of the figure in a two-thirds movement away from the picture plane, lending the same depth to the work. But unlike Vaudechamp, Amans frequently worked in the three-quarter-length pose format, making many of his portraits larger than the 32 x 26 inches layout favored by Vaudechamp and the standard one throughout the period. Amans' works are often minor variations on a general theme of 36 x 30.

Edwin Phelps (1796-1863)
Self Portrait, circa 1835
oil on canvas
25 1/4 x 22 inches
New Orleans Museum of Art, Gift of David Kleck, 85.81

This minor increase in the size of the picture plane is also to be seen in the size of the figure. Amans' figures tend to be larger, bolder, and occupy far more of the space around them, in contrast to the floating, atmospheric backgrounds of the earlier neoclassic

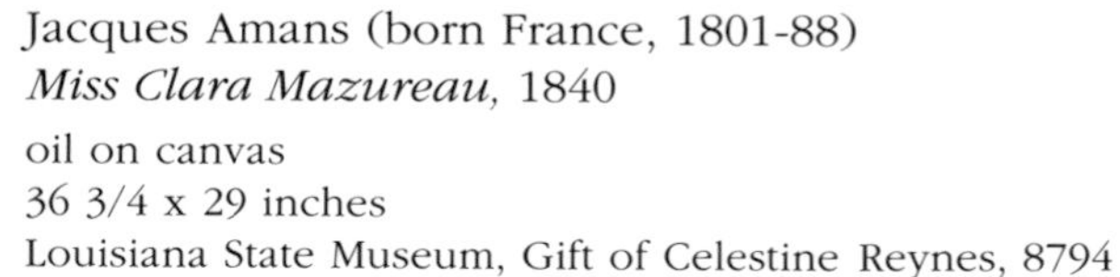

Jacques Amans (born France, 1801-88)
Miss Clara Mazureau, 1840
oil on canvas
36 3/4 x 29 inches
Louisiana State Museum, Gift of Celestine Reynes, 8794

Jacques Amans (born France, 1801-88)
Self Portrait, 1845
oil on canvas
29 1/2 x 26 inches
The Historic New Orleans Collection, 1981.376.4

traditions. Amans' portrait of Clara Mazureau demonstrates the same figurative placement and background distance as can be seen in Vaudechamp's portrait of Claiborne, but the scale of the other anatomical features is not in Vaudechamp's hesitant spirit. The lush modelling and fullness of the arms are an indication of the taste of the Empire period, for Amans is bolder in presenting the attitudes on his subjects' faces, and his figures, like the furniture of Prudent Mallard, take up a lot of room.

Perhaps the paintings should be seen as harbingers, for by the end of Amans' first decade in New Orleans taste in portraiture was undergoing a radical change. The smaller oil portrait was slowly giving way to the photographic image then emerging, and portraiture was becoming far larger, with much greater background detail and more genre elements.

While Amans was in New Orleans he obtained an important public commission to complete a large equestrian portrait of General Jackson. It was to be hung in the mayor's office of the City Hall building, recently completed to the designs of James Gallier. To accomplish the monumental composition, Amans took on the help of an itinerant portrait artist, Theodore Sidney Moise, who had developed a rather facile ability as an animalier. He frequently added images of animals or pets to his paintings of plantation children during his many tours through the South.

Moise was born in Charleston, South Carolina and began his career as an accountant in a cotton brokering firm. According to a brief biographical sketch of the artist written by his son, Moise never really intended to become a painter, and declined the offer of an uncle to send him to Europe for further study. Instead, he pursued the far more respectable and practical career of a cotton broker. "While so doing he painted portraits of his friends, relatives and acquaintances merely as an amateur. From this casual practice he soon became quite proficient and his reputation spread far and wide."[19]

Convinced by now of his abilities, Moise undertook painting as a full-time career and began his itinerancy. He worked in Woodville, Mississippi for at least a year before making his first appearance in New Orleans. Once there he became an established figure of the local art world, and despite continuing his travels to paint portraits, he remained a considerable presence in the cultural life of the city. Although he left New Orleans during the war for service in the Confederate Army, he returned and will figure prominently in the chapter on the academic art of New Orleans in the late nineteenth century.

One of the most important documentable aspects of Moise's career is his rather successful partnerships with other itinerant portrait artists either working in New Orleans, or travelling out from there. In 1842 he worked with James Henry Beard, the Cincinnati artist who wintered in New Orleans. His most extensive partnership was with the Irish academic portraitist Trevor Thomas Fowler. Together they painted a series of portraits using animals and pets as backdrops to the romantic poses of ideally clad children. Throughout the late 1840s they worked together, Fowler rendering the facial likeness and Moise supplying the naturalistic backgrounds. In the late 1850s he worked with Benjamin Franklin Reinhart.

Moise was not restricted to just animals and pets, and his own portrait compositions show that he was a very adept chameleon of portrait styles. Many of his portraits have the flair and verve of French court work during the period, showing his receptivity to the ongoing presence of French culture in the city. Others have a flat, somewhat primitive quality, reminiscent of the early work of George David Coulon. Still others, like his portrait of Mississippi Governor Brandon, echo the poses of American neoclassicism.

The collaboration between Amans and Moise is a reminder of the ongoing importance of the international art world in the portrait circles of New Orleans. Vaudechamp and Amans attracted and

Theodore Sidney Moise (1808-85)
Jeannette and Mary Elizabeth Wells, 1852
oil on canvas
34 x 28 inches
W. T. Hetherwick Collection, Natchitoches, Louisiana

Adolph Rinck (born France, circa 1810)
Charlotte Mathilde Grevenberg du Martait (from Albania Plantation on Bayou Teche), 1843
oil on canvas
32 x 25 1/4 inches
Peter W. Patout Collection, New Orleans

influenced at least two generations of portrait artists and were directly responsible for encouraging several other international artists to come to New Orleans to work. Among these, Adolph Rinck enjoyed one of the greatest successes from 1840 to 1871.

Rinck's training and style indicate a certain shift in the prevailing high styles to which the New Orleans community was now being exposed. Where Amans and Vaudechamp were masters of a certain cool French restraint, Rinck was a student of both the emerging floridity of the French academic salon and the far more pronounced dramatic character focus of the German school. He was, after all, Alsatian, and while he did study with Paul Delaroche in Paris, he also studied and worked at the Berlin Academy in Germany. The proximity of his figures to the picture plane, the fullness of anatomical detail, and the substance in his works have far more in common with the jolly Biedermeier portraits than with the coy restraint of early-nineteenth-century France. One of his recurring props is a turkey feather fan, placed in the hand of his sitter, who is often flourishing it about with considerable grace.

Rinck was not the only artist of note with a German exposure who worked in the city during this time. François Fleischbein was a Bavarian-born artist who worked in the city from 1834 until his death in 1868. Gradually he abandoned portraiture for the new art of commercial portrait photography in the late 1850s. He still painted several portraits whose vivid coloration makes him one of the principal examples of the Biedermeier style in Louisiana.

Fleischbein's compositional approach to the de Berjerac children is a significant omen to developments in Louisiana portraiture in the two decades prior to the war. Painted in 1839, it portends compositions which emerge after the rise of photographic studies. The figures are arranged in a geometrical hierarchy, looking directly

François Fleischbein (born Bavaria, circa 1801/1805-68)
Children of Comte Louis Amedie de Berjerac, 1839
oil on canvas
35 3/4 x 29 inches
Louisiana State Museum, 9461

out from the picture plane with a certain theatrical naivete. It is a complex painting, charming in its ambitious intent. Although slightly larger than the typical head and shoulders format, it seems to be a work in the grand manner due to the full anatomical presentation of the subjects.

Fleischbein painted the de Berjerac children in the very year Louis Daguerre perfected his new mechanical image-taking technique, which he called the "daguerreotype." The appeal of the daguerreotype, and subsequent photographic forms, was immediate and widespread. According to the New Orleans *Times-Picayune* on March 24, 1840, "a young French gentleman [was] engaged in making representations of buildings by a new system invented by Daguerre...."

L. Sotta, (active New Orleans, 1840-42)
Mrs. Leonard Wiltz, 1841
oil on canvas
31 5/8 x 25 inches
Louisiana State Museum, 8415

Henry Byrd (born Ireland, circa 1805/1806-84)
Hattie Lee Kit, 1850
oil on canvas
44 x 33 1/2 inches
Louisiana State Museum, 8672

Thomas Cantwell Healey (1820-89)
Judge Bullard, 1843
oil on canvas
45 3/4 x 38 1/2 inches
Tulane University Art Collection, Gift of the Supreme Court of the State of Louisiana, New Orleans

George David Coulon (born France, 1822-1904)
Boy with Rose, 1842
oil on canvas
22 x 18 inches
Louisiana State Museum, 4931

Once photography became an established means of having a likeness taken for family purposes, the nature and function of portraiture, and those who practiced it, changed forever. Large numbers of itinerant portrait artists, of limited ability, quickly abandoned the brush for the lens and the acid bath. Many of those who did continue to paint portraits now adapted their technique, and their approach to the new public demand for a far more truthful likeness.

Of those artists affected by the rise of photography, the most important example is George David Coulon. Coulon's long tenure as the dean of Louisiana painters began with his efforts as a portraitist in the early 1840s. Several of his early portraits, especially those of children, use the wonderfully subtle convention of placing a rose in clasped hands held out like a modest offering. It is a convention as clearly drawn from print sources as many of the works by Salazar. But the foursquare image of the subjects, with their backs rigidly against the picture plane, is pure photographic studio.

Coulon once remarked, in his brief biographical notes, that "until about 1853 all the portraits I made I painted them direct from nature and from Death Masks...." Coulon's principal biographer has observed that this "curious statement seems to mean that after 1853 he also painted portraits from photographs."[20] By 1872 Coulon was in practice with John Hawley Clark making colored photographs that were difficult to distinguish from previous oil portrait work.

Economic trends and technological advances conspired to create a marked divergence in portrait styles. On the one hand the head and shoulders format of the neoclassical type began a slow decline, still favored by a few old-line traditional families but really in total eclipse by the time the war broke out. On the other hand, there is a parallel, though by no means widespread, rise in the grand manner portrait. These works, far larger in scale than anything previously created in Louisiana, were intended for the great houses being built with the new cotton and sugar money. If we can refer to the earlier works as neoclassical, then surely these great canvases from the two decades prior to the war can be called plantation baroque.

"Louisiana," in the romantic language of Lyle Saxon, "reached its most prosperous period in the twenty years prior to the Civil War. These in truth were 'the good old times.' Plantation-owners reaped fortunes carried from the fertile soil; and the current of the Mississippi carried the commerce of mid-America to the levee at New Orleans."[21] It also carried a new type of portrait artist, with a much deeper academic grounding than the first generation of itinerants and their French counterparts.

Artists like Trevor Thomas Fowler, G. P. A. Healy, and James Henry Wright were offering their clients portraits painted in the new

George P. A. Healy (1813-94, active New Orleans, 1860-61)
Portrait of General Pierre G. T. Beauregard
oil on canvas
59 x 45 inches
City of Charleston, South Carolina Collection

James Henry Wright (1813-83)
Three Children in a Landscape, 1855
oil on canvas
68 x 54 inches
The Lauren Rogers Museum of Art, Laurel, Mississippi

American grand manner. These "portraits in large" were usually 60 x 50 inches, or even bigger. Whether placed in enormous gilded frames sold in the most prominent cabinetmakers' shops, or actually fitted into the woodwork of a home over a mantel or in an entrance hall, they were intended to impress the viewer with wealth and authority, and were far removed from the more humble intentions of the head and shoulder pose.

Practitioners of the plantation baroque portrait-in-the-large included a variety of artists with many skills. Professor William Gerdts has observed that it was a style "that did not attract very many of the more original and creative young artists."[22] As in the previous decades, international artists with considerable academic training continued to make brief visits to New Orleans. Among those, William Rumpler and Francois Bernard were the most exemplary. Bernard's best work is in the sophisticated manner of the French salon, combining a very lush and painterly image with the newly emerging strain of realism.

François Bernard (born France, circa 1812, active New Orleans, 1856-75)
The Ladies of the Orchard Plantation—Paulina De Graffenried and Daughter, Sallie Pickett (Mrs. Robert C. Cummings), 1854
oil on canvas
72 x 60 inches
Francis Stokes Randall Collection, Shreveport, Louisiana

William Rumpler (born Germany, 1824)
Davidson Family, 1858
oil on canvas
66 1/4 x 62 3/4 inches
The Louisiana State Museum, 10824

William Henry Baker (1825-75)
The Carr Children, circa 1855
oil on canvas
60 x 54 1/4 inches
Roger Houston Ogden Collection, New Orleans

Attributed to Robert Gschwindt (born Hungary?, active New Orleans, 1854-67)
Madame Alcee Villere, circa 1858
oil on canvas
46 1/2 x 40 inches
The Historic New Orleans Collection, 1981.376.4

One long-term resident painter in the grand manner was W. H. Baker. Although born in Nashville, Tennessee, Baker's family mercantile business had brought him to New Orleans as early as 1848, and he painted there intermittently until the Civil War. Baker's signature convention was the use of a rather large dog in both individual genre portraits and in his large canvases of children. The dog almost always is stretching its neck up to nuzzle its master.

Baker's contemporary, Robert Gschwindt, brought a genuine breath of the French salon to his sitters in the Vieux Carré. According to the New Orleans *Bee* for December 29, 1854, Gschwindt was "a pupil of the celebrated Thomas Couture, and an artist of high reputation." A man of several talents, and extended occupations, he possessed a "large number of paintings by the old masters" which he offered for sale. He also "takes likenesses, copies old paintings, restores faded ones and reproduces portraits from daguerreotypes." The last reference again confirms the slow demise of portraiture as it struggled to compete with photography.

In April of 1861 war broke out. With the exception of a few military portraits, and a remarkable child's portrait signed and dated by Baker in New Orleans during the war, portrait activity was at a minimum. Portraitists, even as they continued to paint, had other concerns, and some, like B. F. Reinhart, were flagrant partisans of the Confederate cause.

Most standard biographical dictionaries of artists state that Reinhart left New Orleans for England before the outbreak of the war. This supposition is probably due to his northern origins. However, research into the newspaper accounts of the period reveal that he remained in New Orleans, contributing his time and talents to the Confederate armed forces. Between 1861 and the capitulation

Benjamin Franklin Reinhart (1827-85)
Sally Pope, 1859
oil on canvas
52 1/2 x 44 inches
Caroline R. Pack Collection, on loan to Magnolia Hall, Natchez, Mississippi

Richard Clague (born France, 1821-73)
Portrait of Mrs. Henry de Brueys, 1862
oil on canvas
36 x 29 inches
New Orleans Museum of Art, Ella West Freeman Foundation Matching Fund, 72.37

Richard Clague (born France, 1821-73)
Portrait of Henry Clement de Brueys, 1862
oil on canvas
36 x 29 inches
New Orleans Museum of Art, Ella West Freeman Foundation Matching Fund, 72.36

Richard Clague (born France, 1821-73)
Portrait of Edward de Brueys, 1862
oil on canvas
30 x 25 inches
New Orleans Museum of Art, Ella West Freeman Foundation Matching Fund, 72.38

of New Orleans on May 1, 1862, he contributed money and painted portraits for the Southern cause. Indeed, a troop of soldiers, under the command of Col. Frank Bartlett, was called the Reinhart Guards in honor of the support of "this most public spirited citizen," as the *Daily Delta* for February 14, 1862 called him. He fled New Orleans for London at the time of the capitulation, but once there continued his efforts by painting a portrait of General Lee, again taken from a daguerreotype.

During the course of the war Richard Clague, whose significance as a landscape artist far overshadows his work as a portraitist, painted a group of works which represent the most important pieces of realist portraiture in the history of Louisiana art. Clague's broodingly intense self-portrait is an honest revelation of his brilliant, complex being, a being trained in the highest traditions of the French Barbizon school. Independent, unable to settle into either a specific locale or into a marriage with his longtime mistress, Clague drifted through the war years in and out of uniform. He briefly served in the Confederate army, and then returned to Louisiana to live with his cousins, the de Brueys family.

Perhaps during his stay with them in 1862 he painted all four members of the household. None were spared the relentless honesty of his penetrating brush. Madame de Brueys is a matron with a slightly drooping chin and mature gaze. Monsieur de Brueys' eyes burn with a dark intensity, and a quiet war-weary gaze.

These images are a fitting conclusion to one of the most productive periods in the history of art in Louisiana. Our discussions have considered a small handful of the scores of artists active in the city. The images of the citizens which they have left behind are important material culture, indications of the assimilation of various strains of style, even as the very sitters at hand were being drawn into the expanding life of the American nation. After the war, portraiture would continue along more prescribed academic lines, and would be commissioned by a far smaller segment of the community.

All the subsequent paintings we shall see were created as ornamentation, or in the artist's burst of deeply personal creativity. To leave behind portraiture is to leave behind the very people of the past itself, frozen in time. They gaze down from domestic or institutional walls, or molder on racks in hidden storage vaults or behind the painting dealers' more saleable wares.

CHAPTER THREE

Light in Louisiana Landscape Art

LIGHT IN LOUISIANA LANDSCAPE art breaks through the panoramas of the early scenic artists to shine with dramatic intensity upon the poetic, luminescent efforts of the painters working in mid-century. Then it sets in the murky glow of formulaic fetid swamps and distant bayous. At certain moments in this metaphoric day, Louisiana landscape art achieves a truly indigenous grasp of the visual potentials of the surrounding countryside. The fulfillment of this potential is to be seen in many of the works created by some of the best artists who have ever worked in the state.

Apart from topographical views and the somewhat crude drawings and watercolors of several amateur artists, there is no precedent for the rise of Louisiana landscape art which corresponds to developments in portraiture. George David Coulon makes a reference to "a good Spanish landscape painter Romegas," who may have worked in New Orleans as early as 1772. Unlike Salazar, however, there are no extant works by him, and he seems to have made little impact.[1]

Landscape art was not in great demand, a trend often lamented by artists throughout the new world. Portraiture dominated the visual arts, and those landscape works which were created, as over-mantel decorations or parlor ornaments, were far rarer than the ubiquitous likeness dominating the middle-class home. When landscape art did begin to emerge in the national culture, its first presence can be seen, not unsurprisingly, as background details in portraits with allegorical as well as documentary intentions.

However, once landscape art became an obsession amongst a close and highly influential group of painters in the northeast, it took on a position of great importance in the intellectual establishment of the country. From this vantage it entered the popular consciousness. This penetration can be "heard" in the lavish journalistic descriptions of landscape works seen in Louisiana.

As is often the case with nineteenth-century aesthetics, theories of landscape painting swung continually between two strongly defined polarities. On the one hand, certain notions present in the artistic community since the Renaissance perpetuated the idea that the purpose of landscape art was to enlighten and inspire by creating a world visibly occupied with allegorical conventions. The setting sun, the vanishing perspective leading to a central point, the worker in the field, and well-defined tree in all stages of growth are the accepted elements of this school. This approach would find many adherents in Louisiana, where the swamp, the bayou, and the moss-hung tree assumed a similar essential function.

However, counterbalancing the fanciful and formulaic approach to the landscape were the concerns of the realists, both romantic and naturalistic, who saw in landscape painting an opportunity for more profound philosophic speculation. Truth and beauty were preoccupations of the nineteenth-century imagination, whether seen in a glorious sunset or in a life of noble virtue. The high priest of "truth" in landscape art was the English writer John Ruskin.

Ruskin's books, especially *Modern Painters,* declared that any true greatness in art lies in the artist's ability to respond accurately and sensitively to the real beauty inherent in nature. Ruskin admonishes the viewer who felt that a high regard for landscape art would "lead him at once into fields of fond imagination, and may have been surprised to find that the following of beauty brought him always under a sterner dominion of mysterious law; that brightness was continually based on obedience, and all majesty only another form of submission."[2] Only rarely would the Louisiana landscape artists either submit or obey, but when they did, as in the case of the school of Clague, important close observations of the native scene were the result.

Writing in an exhibition catalog on the first landscape painting created in this country, Edward J. Nygren speaks of the "unusual opportunity" created by the geographic and cultural isolation of the New World. "America provides an unusual opportunity to explore how depictions of real and ideal landscapes reflected changing attitudes toward nature and became symbols of social concepts."[3] This assessment of the possibilities of charting "the emergence of artistic conventions" is especially pertinent to the study of Louisiana landscape painting.

By the late nineteenth century, several artists had produced the standard "vocabulary" for the Louisiana scene. This scene consisted of "moss draped oaks, sleepy bayous, swamps teeming with wildlife, lakes dotted with cypress knees, waving green ribbons of sugar cane alongside fields dotted with cotton, venerable houses mixed in with cajun cottages and sharecropper's cabins."[4] The high drama of this description is most appropriate. The first landscape artists in Louisiana were far more occupied with creating scenic panoramas to lure a paying public, or painting backdrop scenery in the many local theatres, than they were with evoking those divisions between the real and the ideal which Nygren, and many other art historians, see as the principal characteristic of landscape art in the period.

The first recorded landscape artist to establish a lasting public impression was Toussaint François Bigot, a native of Rennes, Brittany, France. Bigot first appeared in New Orleans in 1816, when, according to at least one account, he was twenty-two. Throughout his career, Bigot alternated between painting scenes and teaching. Coulon observes that Bigot, "who painted many Louisiana views...had been a teacher of drawing in the College of Rennes."

In 1826 Bigot painted a series of views of the Place d'Armes and surrounding buildings which was exhibited at the "Cosmorama" on the corner of Orleans and Bourbon streets. The proprietors of this establishment were sure the "views will be highly interesting" to the public, "in as much as they are calculated to recall to their minds the most glorious recollections." Bigot's paintings were also praised in the same article for "correctness of delineation and...finish of the work."[5]

Nostalgia is not only a fundamental ingredient in the reviewer's regard for this work, but also for all future Louisiana landscape art. The northeast painters, especially those in the Hudson River School, balanced recollection with sincere regard, but the Louisiana painter would always tend towards a more moody evocation of the local scene. While this tendency is apparent in some of the earlier works, with their theatrical associations, it becomes a concern of near religious proportions for the artists painting in the late nineteenth century.

Ironically enough, Bigot was painting his panoramas at precisely the same moment that John Vanderlyn, the legendary history painter, was eking out a small living as an itinerant portrait artist in the French Quarter. How Vanderlyn must have felt if he viewed Bigot's far more primitive works is a tantalizing point for historical speculation. Just seven years earlier Vanderlyn had completed his monumental view of the gardens and palace of Versailles, which had been set into a special exhibition hall in New York City. Public interest in panoramas of this type may very well have provided an incentive to Bigot and subsequent generations of Southern panoramists.

"Correctness of delineation" is a somewhat ironic description of Bigot's work, for there is a spirit of protorealism in those which have survived. *Alchapalaia, Louisiana* has many of the characteristics of the emerging American allegorical landscape art tradition, especially to be seen in the trees living and dead which line the foreground. However, the consistency of the light quality, and the distance of the background grove, do little to heighten the theatrical quality of the work. The companion painting, *Alligator Hunting,* presents a rather squalid rural setting totally devoid of the romantic notions of the landscape prevalent in the immediate antebellum period.

By the time Bigot had painted these works, in the late 1840s, at least one other artist had appeared in Louisiana, following the same itinerary as many of his contemporaries in the portrait field. Robert Brammer was an Irish-born artist who worked in Louisville, Kentucky, in partnership with the painter Augustus Von Smith. Together they painted a well-known view of the Oakland House and Race Course. Brammer begins to appear in city directories in New Orleans in 1842, and remains a consistent presence in the city until his death in 1853.

Brammer's landscape painting seems to have been his only artistic outlet, indicating that tastes of the day were high enough to support an artist. According to the *Daily Orleanian,* which praised him as "an artist of rare attainments," he was "seldom or never unengaged."

Brammer's style is defined by the same journal as one in which "the blended hues...are so perfect" that the viewer is left "in doubt as to whether he is looking on a picture, or an ideal creation, or reality itself." Journalistic excess aside, this view is evidence of growing public interest in the fine points of truth in nature, the primary symbolic concept of the age.

Brammer's landscapes invariably use the same formulaic approach to trees and "blended hues." His coloration consists of juxtaposing faint primary colors against a diffuse sky. Greens and browns predominate, and there seems to be little interest in any actual recording of wildlife or plant materials. The most distinguishing element in the pictures is the manner in which he brushes in the details of the leaves, for they are painted with a rocaille brushstroke that is distinctly European in origin and feel.

Bigot's and Brammer's works are rather singular isolated examples of landscape art in an area where an indigenous form, or stylistic convention, had yet to develop. Their contemporaries in the field were often set decorators or church muralists, like Leon Pomerade, whose works in the St. Louis Cathedral were much admired. Pomerade exhibited a panorama in November of 1849, and painted portraits throughout his career.

At least one local set decorator's attempted landscape art reflected the romantic infatuation with natural light in transition. L. D. G. Develle worked at the Orleans Theatre for more than thirty

Toussaint François Bigot (born France, 1794-1869)
Alchapalaia, Louisiana
28 1/2 x 36 inches
Mrs. George Holden Collection, San Francisco

Robert Brammer (born Ireland, circa 1811-53)
Louisiana Landscape
oil on canvas
29 x 36 inches
The Collection of Jay P. Altmayer, Mobile, Alabama

years. He first appears in the newspaper accounts on March 24, 1829 with a notice for the decorations he painted for a performance of the opera *Marie*. The last notices of him appear in 1866, when it is announced that he will give lessons in his home or studio.

Develle's set decorations have long since disappeared, and he would really be of little interest as a landscape painter were it not that his greatest surviving work, *French Market and Red Store,* was such an important example of creative developments in the use of natural light in Louisiana landscape art. The painting features an intense burning light which we have come to associate with the luminist movement. Together with a work by the obscure artist Matthew Kirsh, called *Romantic Landscape* and painted in New Orleans in 1854, it demonstrates an awareness on the part of the local art community of an important national trend.

Matthew Kirsh (circa 1839-91)
Romantic Landscape, 1854
oil on canvas
29 1/4 x 36 3/4 inches
Louisiana State Museum, 4907

Luminism is the descriptive term that art historians have given to works of art which display a heightened awareness of the effects of light and air upon bodies of water at transitional times of day. It was first defined, and given a name, by the art historian John I. H. Baur in 1954. As a descriptive and interpretive term it has most often been applied to the works of the first and second generations of the Hudson River School.[6]

For Baur, and for many who have subsequently chosen to use the term *luminism* as a philosophic, rather than a merely descriptive term, light in a work of art is a means of illuminating the artist's ultimate technical tribute to the scene at hand. He presents it for ideal contemplation by removing himself as an obvious interpreter. Barbara Novak has described this process as being "so powerful that the artist's feeling is transferred directly to the object, with no sense of the artist as intermediary."[7]

Relative to the development of an American landscape art is the central role the artist often chose to play. This could be done by projecting a personal style and a distinctly personal vision upon the landscape. Thomas Cole is the great mediating figure between those landscape artists who followed the allegorical efforts of Claude Lorraine and invented imaginary landscapes as a setting for moral or mythic fable, and those artists who were genuinely interested in the actual substance of the available, local setting.

Cole's use of clear natural light is the first example in this country of an international trend. German romantic landscape art of the first quarter of the nineteenth century possesses the same clarity, the same dispassionate evocation of a highly passionate scene. Ironically, many painters in the luminist mode have been criticized for creating scenes of tremendous fantasy when, in reality, they were honestly depicting certain spectacular effects of natural light.

Luminism was not a self-conscious theory propounded or taught in any way by artists, writers, or critics working in the North or the South. However, Northern writers like Ralph Waldo Emerson and Henry David Thoreau, and Southern artists and editors like T. Addison Richards and J. D. B. deBow, expressed, in profoundly different language, a reverence for nature approaching deification.

Transcendentalism, as articulated by Thoreau and Emerson in particular, had moved the seat of the Godhead from a distant height to the local forest. A fervent pantheism can be detected in many contemporary accounts and responses to nature. Already, in the case of the Northern landscape, there is the suggestion that nature may be the most suitable refuge for the mind weary from the demands of the capitalist/industrial society rapidly emerging there. In the South, nature, as the site of the agrarian economy, was far more immediate. Concerns about the land, as expressed in the pages of *DeBow's Literary Review,* were focused upon saving a rapidly deteriorating soil bank.

Both transcendental philosophy and luminist painting were Northern phenomena alien to the Southern mentality. Religious attitudes in the South remained either fundamentally Protestant or didactically Catholic. Appreciation of the beauties of the local scenery was often expressed in the self-conscious letters being exchanged between plantations, but was hardly articulated in depth in extended publications. One notable exception in this somewhat barren field was the Southern landscape artist T. Addison Richards.

Richards was a Georgia native who had published a volume, with his brother, illustrating the wonders of the Georgia countryside, called *Georgia Illustrated.* Ten years later, in 1853, Richards published an article called "The Landscape of the South" in *Harper's New Monthly Magazine.* It sharply defined the critical and artistic distinctions between the landscape of the North and South:

> For the verdant meadows of the North, dotted with cottages and grazing herds, the South has her broad savannahs, calm in the shadow of the palmetto and the magnolia: or the magnificence of the Hudson, the Delaware and the Susquehanna, are her mystical lagunes, in whose stately arcades of cypress, fancy floats at will through all the wilds of past and future.[8]

Richards' challenge to artists north and south to begin exploring the visual possibilities of the Southern scene was met in two places, the Great Dismal Swamp of Virginia and North Carolina, and increasingly after 1850, in Louisiana.

Develle's *French Market and Red Store* may simply be the product of an artist who depended upon the effects of theatrical lighting. The work has a glow similar to the flaming footlights that satisfied an audience desperate for cheap thrills. Develle's contemporary, Hippolyte Sebron, is not subject to the same critique. He was an artist whose awareness of the importance and effect of natural light was compounded by his personal familiarity with the new technique of daguerreotypes as well as his abilities in the European luminist tradition.

Giant Steamboats on the Levee at New Orleans, which was painted in the Crescent City in 1853, is one of the first genuinely luminescent works to be painted in Louisiana. The light which falls upon the levee and the steamboats is at once atmospheric and allegorical. As filtered through the smoke of the steamships it casts a warm glow upon a scene of economic prosperity, while infusing the scene with the actual transfiguring light of the sun as it sets in the west and reflects upon the lake, bayous, canals, and river which surround the city.

Sebron's tenure in Louisiana was relatively brief. He was thought to have been in residence only in the years between 1850 and 1854.

Louis Dominique Grandjean Develle (born France, circa 1799-1868)
French Market and Red Store, between 1829 and 1850
oil on canvas
35 1/8 x 51 5/8 inches
The Historic New Orleans Collection

Hippolyte Sebron (born France, 1801-79)
Giant Steamboats on the Levee at New Orleans, 1853
oil on canvas
48 1/2 x 72 3/8 inches
Tulane University Art Collection, New Orleans, Gift of D. H. Holmes Company, New Orleans

Recently, however, a painting has come to light called *Crocodile Lake, Louisiana,* signed and dated 1861. Whether Sebron painted the work in Louisiana or upon his return to France is unclear.

What is dazzlingly visible is Sebron's masterful manipulation of luminism to capture the scene. The golden light cast upon the lakeshore and the trunks of the surrounding trees has the same quality of fantastic realism apparent in many Hudson River works, especially those of Fitz Hugh Lane and Frederic Edwin Church. The gradations of light—from the deep blue of the empyrean to the warm orange of the tree line dissolving in the diminishing light of the setting sun—are a convention which will reappear in subsequent Louisiana landscape painting, especially that of Charles Giroux.

By the 1850s the artistic community of Louisiana would have had an ample exposure to luminist landscape art. As early as 1845 the portrait itinerant entrepreneur George Cooke had opened a gallery on the third story of 13 St. Charles Street. As the New Orleans *Daily Tropic* for September 22, 1845 notes, "he has a number of landscapes from the pencils of Cole, Chapman & Doughty...."

Louisiana landscape enthusiasts would also have had ample exposure to Frederic Edwin Church, the premier landscape artist of the American scene. Not only was Church's monumental *Niagara Falls* noticed with great favor in the local papers, but was made available in engraved form as well. It also seems possible that a version of *Niagara Falls* was exhibited in a room over Bloomfield & Steele's bookstore, next to the *Picayune* office at 60 Camp Street.[9] That work was praised for the "presence of a stupendous reality, with the abstraction of motion and sound." Church's frequent trips to South America and to Mexico must have taken him through New Orleans on several occasions. On at least one of these he made the acquaintance of the family of writer Grace King, which she mentions in her memoirs.

Nor were these artists the only Hudson River School painters present in the city. James Robb, a local collector, lent many works to Cooke's gallery and was one of his principal backers. Robb had also commissioned Asher Brown Durand to paint two works for his personal collection, "two paintings representing morning and evening," which were prominently hung in his entrance hall.[10] One of these, *Forenoon,* is now in the collection of the New Orleans Museum of Art.

By a rather intriguing coincidence, during the same time Durand was working on the Robb commission he was also president of the National Academy of Design, thus helping to set the tone of landscape art when the young artist Joseph Rusling Meeker was a student. Meeker was a native of Newark, New Jersey, and had grown up in Auburn, New York. He would become the foremost articulator of the romantic Louisiana landscape art in the nineteenth century.

Like T. Addison Richards, Meeker found it very difficult to establish himself as a landscape artist. An absence of taste for landscape painting is a fact which was noted in an 1878 account of the artist which found "the taste for art, notably landscapes, was not pronounced here, but there were a few who were willing to give remunerative prices for such pictures."[11]

By 1861 he had moved west to St. Louis in search of new scenery to paint and a new audience to help support him. When the war started he enlisted in the Federal forces, becoming paymaster on a Union gunboat. He was stationed in Louisiana throughout the war, and while there made those series of sketches upon which he based so much of his subsequent artwork. Once the war was over and Meeker returned to St. Louis, he began to paint a series of works which combine the literary allusions of Henry Wadsworth Longfellow and Walt Whitman with his own personal artistic vision.

Meeker's idol, in the true Ruskinian spirit of the age, was not a contemporary Hudson River School artist, but rather the English painter J. W. M. Turner, an appreciation he articulates at length in an article for *The Western* in 1878. Therein he gives a most revealing insight into some of the most substantive techniques and motivations of any artist working in the period. Meeker found in Turner's art a point of visual "repose" which redeemed the sense of isolation and despair which were the primary allegorical ingredients of his own landscape art.[12] Like Turner, Meeker's colors are "disposed so as to produce the utmost harmony; and the major and minor lights and shades are so arranged that the tone of the works shall give a satisfying sense of completeness—a high light there, a lesser light there, and so on through the scale, repeating a like gradation in the darks, and at last carrying the eye by deft combinations of line and tone to the final element of repose beyond all."

The Victorian verbiage of this description should not mislead the viewer into confusing Meeker's compositions with the work of the master he so admired. Much of Meeker's work has a strong defined foreground, and a softly suggested background, which are arranged so as to create a wide expanse in the mid-ground where bodies of water provide the reflective light source. Like his Hudson River contemporaries, Meeker often imbues a tree with a spirit of pathetic fallacy, allowing it to become a kind of central character. Trees living and trees decayed and dead are juxtaposed in typical nineteenth-century allegorical fashion, subtle reminders of the cycles of life in nature.

Meeker's true genius as a painter rests in his ability to create a vivid image of light and shadow. Feeling that a "quality of mystery" was "essential to the completeness of a picture," Meeker paints with a highly defined vocabulary of color. Interaction of primary and secondary shades are crucial to his work, for "understanding the

Joseph Rusling Meeker (1827-87)
Louisiana Dawn, 1866
oil on canvas
14 x 20 inches
Roger Houston Ogden Collection, New Orleans

Joseph Rusling Meeker (1827-87)
Bayou Plaquemines, 1881
oil on canvas
20 1/2 x 36 inches
Roger Houston Ogden Collection, New Orleans

value of this," the artist "vaguely defines such of his outlines as would offend the eye by their boldness, and by the use of mists and nimbus clouds lending obscurity to portions of the picture suggestive of...vistas."

Bayou Plaquemines may have been created with an appreciation for Turner, but in spirit and effect it echoes the power and authority of Frederic Edwin Church's *Twilight in the Wilderness.* The huge canopy of clouds are on fire with the last light of day thrown up from the sun, which will soon vanish into the murky, all-consuming swamp. Foreshortening is arranged so that the sky is flattened against the picture plane, and the receding coloration of the vaguely defined background heightens the depth and perspective. This does indeed obscure the central axis of the vanishing perspective, blending all into the attitude of repose which Meeker so admired.

"Every artist ought to paint what he himself loves," Meeker wrote, for if his love may "be pure and sweetly to him, what he loves will be lovely." Meeker obviously loved what he saw in the swamps of Louisiana and along the banks of the Yazoo River in Mississippi. More than any other artist of his time, he was responsible for creating for the nation's public the haunting image of the single moss-hung oak, the one of Whitman's poem, "I Saw in Louisiana a Live Oak Growing."

While Whitman may very well have seen a live oak growing on his trip to New Orleans in 1848 Meeker did not see the heroine he pursues as relentlessly as she pursued her own lost love. The legend and poetry of the Evangeline myth fascinated Meeker, and he created a series of works which dealt in specific and symbolic terms with her story.[13] Often he paints a single tree, sharply defined against the very surface of the picture plane, moss-hung or trailing coiled vines, which he calls the "Evangeline tree." Behind this tree we can just glimpse a diffused background of blue-green or grey-green harmonies composed as rows of distant trees. That this proved a rather successful formula is apparent by the quantity of works in this style which survive. However, Meeker also created two specific works, of far greater originality, which illustrate the mood and spirit of Longfellow's epic romance of the Acadian diaspora.

The Acadians in the Atchafalaya, "Evangeline" was the first of these works, painted in 1871. True to Longfellow's poem, if not to actual historical circumstance, the "cumbrous boat, that was rowed by the Acadian boatmen" is seen making its way down the "golden stream of the broad and swift Mississippi." Rather like the dwarfing landscapes of Claude Lorraine, the scene is far vaster than the small boat, and the tiny heroine is but a suggested presence.

An enormous live oak spans the foreground like a grotesque baroque proscenium. Creeping around its trunk is trumpet vine, in

Joseph Rusling Meeker (1827-87)
The Acadians in the Atchafalaya, "Evangeline," 1871
oil on canvas
32 1/8 x 42 3/16 inches
The Brooklyn Museum, A. Augustus Healy Fund, 50.118

Joseph Rusling Meeker (1827-87)
The Land of Evangeline, 1874
oil on canvas
33 x 45 1/2 inches
The St. Louis Art Museum, Gift of Mrs. W. P. Edgerton by exchange

Meyer Straus (born Germany, 1831-1905, active New Orleans, 1869-72)
Bayou Teche
oil on canvas
30 x 60 inches
Southeastern Newspaper Corporation Collection on loan to the Morris Museum of Art, Augusta, Georgia

full bloom, and the requisite moss drapes its limbs, waving, in Longfellow's words, "like banners that hung on the walls of ancient cathedrals." Throughout this cathedral domain of live oak and water lily a golden light falls.

The 1874 companion painting, *The Land of Evangeline,* helps complete the story. Here Meeker has employed a far more obvious vanishing perspective, for on the right side of the picture plane the eye is led down a long alley symbolic of Evangeline's eternal search for her lost Gabriel. Like the tree beneath which she sleeps, Evangeline may now be nearly dead from exhaustion, and yet taking hope from nature, she sleeps, and "the dawn of an opening heaven/ Lighted her soul in sleep with the glory of regions celestial."

While the air of Meeker's swamps may be more filled with the smell of Victorian sentiment than the "baneful effluvia" which Audubon describes, they do set an important precedent. The romantic moss-hung live oak will become an enduring compositional convention in Louisiana painting, outlasting criticism, changing technique, and even the tides of taste. Finally it becomes the ultimate artistic parody, still hanging proudly for sale on the iron railing of Jackson Square.

Before that occurs, however, a singular yet brilliant strain of pictorial realism will emerge in Louisiana painting, created by Richard Clague. Clague's landscape art was first created in the high noon of old South prosperity, and endured the transition of war and reconstruction to spawn a lasting artistic legacy. Before Clague began to paint, landscape art in Louisiana was little more than a symbolic expression. Like the theatrical backdrops of Develle, or his follower Meyer Straus, Clague's precedents and contemporaries were far more prone to certain literary and allegorical motivations than to actual observation.

In his life and art Richard Clague embodied the conflicting heritage of the French and American schools in New Orleans. He was of mixed parentage, his father being a native of the Isle of Man in England and his mother being a descendent of an old Creole clan. It was her family, the de la Roches, who provided the young artist with cultural exposure and means to pursue an education in art after his parents' divorce in 1832.[14] From that point Clague divided his time between New Orleans and Paris, which accounts for the international flavor of his style.

Clague's youthful itinerancy included periods of study in Switzerland and Paris during the nascence of French Barbizon painting. He also spent some time in New Orleans working as an assistant to the muralist Leon Pomerade. It was during the 1850s that Clague reached his maturity as an artist. His return to New Orleans is a critical event, for it is really at this time that the truly indigenous school of Louisiana landscape art begins.

By exposure and cultural inclination Clague was more influenced by French Barbizon art than by the ideal, intellectual creations of the Hudson River School. Barbizon painters like Narcisse Diaz de la Pena, Jean-Baptise Camille Corot, and Jean-François Millet sought to portray nature in its more coarse and basic reality. Their reality depicted the life of peasants bound to a landscape exhausted by agricultural exploitation, and devoid of scenery worthy of highly colored exaltation.

One senses in the Barbizon school a fierce avant-garde spirit, making them among the first nonconformist artists. The French nobleman Count Nieuwerkerke spoke of their art as "painting of democrats, of those who don't change their linen...." Politically, they championed the rights and virtues of the peasant class. Visually, they preferred the realities of the French countryside to the sentiments of a bourgeois materialistic court, crumbling under the weight of the Second Empire.

Philosophically, the hidden agenda of the Barbizon artist involved a troubled confrontation with the changes in the European landscape wrought by the industrial revolution. Peter Bermingham, in his assessment of the impact of this group on American painting, has concluded that "the effort to memorialize essential verities of the natural world in the face of accelerating change" was one manifestation of the essentially conservative mentality of the Barbizon artist.[15]

Richard Clague (born France, 1821-73)
Self Portrait, 1850
oil on canvas
25 1/2 x 21 inches
Louisiana State Museum, 8847

These artists combined a distrust of change with a radical understanding of the subtle possibilities of natural light cast upon a scene of humble origin. Thus they were able to add "to the narrower but no less important formal concerns of the landscape painter in the nineteenth century." Within the larger body of late-nineteenth-century American landscape art, this impulse may be seen in the rather somber tonalist efforts of artists as diverse as J. Francis Murphy and George Inness.

Clague's oft gloomy art in the Barbizon mood predicts later American developments. Perhaps his efforts were leavened by the approach of a devastating war, in which he participated, and which destroyed much of the existing order into which he had been born. During the last years of his life, and for the brief period of the radical Reconstruction of Louisiana under the Federal government, pictorial realism flourished as an artistic style.

Nascent interest in pictorial realism is obvious in the hauntingly penetrating self-portrait Clague painted in 1850. It is a clear demonstration of his familiarity with select demimonde tastes of Paris. That familiarity would be greatly sharpened when Clague accompanied the de Lesseps expedition down the Nile in 1856. With a pronounced drafting skill and keen eye, Clague was taken on as an "artiste photographe" and charged with illustrating the dispatches of the expedition.

Photography was just beginning to come into the artistic consciousness, bringing elements of realism that transcended the affectations of style, resulting in genuine visual documents. Parallel intentions between the Barbizon contemplation of the sublime and mundane, and the truly documentary impulses of the first photographers yielded a new current of art. Landscape painting moved out of a poetic, lyrical mode, however "naturalistically" oriented, and into a style that can be closely associated with the realist movement in literature and politics. In France this may be seen in the works of Emile Zola and Victor Hugo, and in Louisiana by the works of George Washington Cable which outraged most of his contemporaries.

Clague returned to New Orleans in 1857, never to visit or work in France again. When the war broke out he actually enlisted in the company of Marigny de Mandeville, whose dashing portrait epitomizes the flamboyant spirit of the antebellum era. Following Clague's brief tenure in the Confederate Army he took up residence with his Creole cousins, the de Brueys, painting portraits of each in a startlingly unflattering realistic style. Whether he was convalescent in this period, or simply drifting, is unclear, but traditional interpretations of the artist's life do not match the specific biographical details. He seems to have wandered from the home of his cousins to his studio, while at the same time involving himself in a relationship with Pauline Touzé which resulted in an illegitimate child, brought up in France, whom he may never have seen.

All the while he was listing himself as a portraitist at various addresses in the Vieux Carré and Treme sections of the city. A watercolor of the old Treme market painted in 1863 has a highly photographic quality. In particular, the contrasting shadings render the perspective in a chiaroscuro more akin to the daguerreotype than to the dazzling sunlight of New Orleans.

Despite listing himself as a portraitist, Clague continued to pursue, with increasing brilliance, his own personally developed landscape conventions. During the years immediately following the war at least two formats become apparent, both based on less than picturesque elements of the Louisiana countryside: the trappers' cabins on the north shore of Lake Pontchartrain and the shanties along the Mississippi River battures and levees. He often painted on the Algiers side of the river, where he went to live in 1873. This move would prove lethal, for once there he contracted hepatitis under circumstances that can only have been squalid at best, and he died.

Clague's landscapes are not essays on the mood, mystery, and romance of the Louisiana swamps and bayous. They are detailed studies of the countryside, rendered with minute brushstrokes on a dark and heavy ground. Occasionally there are brilliant passages of light, as in the minimal cabin pictures where the mass of the

Richard Clague (born France, 1821-73)
Trapper's Cabin, Manchac, 1870
oil on canvas
14 x 20 inches
Roger Houston Ogden Collection, New Orleans

Richard Clague (born France, 1821-73)
Landscape: Mandeville, Louisiana, circa 1870
oil on canvas
29 1/2 x 41 1/2 inches
Private Collection, New Orleans

cabin is relieved by the juxtaposition of a flattened sky and a receding landscape. But in these works one cannot really feel that light has a metaphoric significance, but rather an illuminating power taken from the proximity of the lake and the brilliant quality of the light itself. As with some luminist works, if poetry is to be found in this light, it is the poetry that exists in the world and not in the artist's imagination.

Certain of Clague's works have a luminist intensity, especially those done during a visit to Spring Hill, Alabama in 1871. The pink skies and fluffy clouds which pass over the decrepit cabins and muddy banks offer a curious contrast. In at least one of the large-scale Clague works, *Landscape: Mandeville, Louisiana,* there is a reddish glow across the horizon line, but any mythic intent of this is more than relieved by the simplicity of the scene, wherein a horse-drawn cart and laborer pass a rather ordinary farm under a vast canopy of live oaks. Clague's most monumental work, a huge scene of the north shore of Lake Pontchartrain, is really amongst his least inspired. The palette is all grey-green, and even in a somber Barbizon mood he has allowed no golden glow of light to relieve a scene uniformly lit by a harsh consistent sun. To find the artist's true genius one must look at the smaller pictures from the Algiers series.

Of those, *Back of Algiers* is the most inspired and the least accurately interpreted. Considering the plight of Louisiana throughout Reconstruction, *Back of Algiers* should not be regarded with the kind of quaint antiquarian interest it has endured in recent exhibitions. Like Marshall Smith's *Bayou Farm,* it is a squalid scene of decay, with derelict structures set in a landscape of ruin. Sugar and cotton slowly declined, and the yeoman farmer, as well as the

Richard Clague (born France, 1821-73)
Back of Algiers, circa 1870-73
oil on canvas
13 3/4 x 20 inches
New Orleans Museum of Art, Gift of Eugenia V. Harrod in memory of her husband, Major Benjamin Morgan Harrod, 13.5

Marshall J. Smith, Jr. (1854-1923)
Bayou Farm
oil on canvas
17 x 36 1/4 inches
New Orleans Museum of Art, Gift of William E. Groves, 66.22

planter, suffered. Despite Grace King's genteel demur that "the times were not hard, they were simply inexorable in their exactions," economic if not spiritual depression was as obvious as Clague's cowshed.

Writing of this period in the larger realm of American landscape painting, John Wilmerding has provided an assessment that rings especially true in the South, where the culture was torn "between drama and calm, clarity of ideals and melancholy meditations on loss, one period of history and art left behind and another uneasily unfolding."[16] At this juncture it would be most satisfying to summarize Clague's career as one of profound transition from the theatrical backdrops and panoramas of early Louisiana to a golden age of light in landscape art. However, while that conclusion might be drawn by an enthusiastic antiquarian/collector, it would give the serious connoisseur pause for considerable reflection.

Clague's legacy as a landscape painter has been a subject for grave misinterpretation. Roulhac Toledano, in her critical evaluation of the artist prepared for the important monographic exhibition of his work in 1974, stated that Clague's adaptation of French Barbizon mannerisms in "composition, style and technique to the depiction of Louisiana resulted in the foundation of a native landscape tradition which lasted for over seventy-five years." This observation is only correct if one credits Clague for elevating the painting of Louisiana landscapes from an amusing adjunct to painting portraits to a full-fledged branch of the arts which the public began to acquire. While Clague's few students, and many imitators, were often capable of producing powerful landscapes, various necessities seem to have compelled them to create large quantities of endlessly repetitive portraits that were popular in the antebellum period. Ultimately, it is tempting to regard the statement of the New Orleans *Bee* for November 30, 1873, in Clague's obituary, as damning, prophetic truth, for it may be that "what he did will live almost as a school itself."

Precisely how true that statement is may be seen in the works of Clague's most obvious followers, Marshall J. Smith, Jr., and William Henry Buck. Both began by painting works in the realist mood of Clague, works which reflected the spirit of Reconstruction Louisiana. Yet both concluded their careers by clinging to a formulaic landscape of vanishing perspective and moss-hung live oaks that often seems to be a repetitive parody relieved only occasionally by natural light.

Of these two artists, Smith was more obviously influenced by Clague. Smith was born in Norfolk, Virginia and raised in New Orleans. Following the war he spent some time studying in Virginia, but he returned to New Orleans in 1869 and studied with Clague. By 1873, the year of Clague's death, he had held his first exhibition.

Clague's impact on Smith was in many respects compounded by the senior artist's death. Marshall Smith, Sr., acquired Clague's sketchbooks for young Smith from the artist's estate. These were used as compositional sources for a series of paintings which Smith executed in Clague's exact compositional format.[17] However, Smith's scenes are far more brightly colored than Clague's and there is an absence of depth and perspective which can be ascribed to their mimetic quality. What Smith really failed to grasp from Clague's sketches, and apparently from observing his works, is the subtle use of shades of color, and the buildup of paint in the architectonic areas of the work to create true visual distinctions between the forms of the structures and atmospheric elements of the landscape.

Smith's own personal style begins to emerge following his important trip to Europe in 1873-74. While there Smith studied in Rome and at the Royal Bavarian Academy in Munich, during the same time that a fellow American artist, Frank Duveneck, was also a student. Upon his return he began to paint a series of landscape works which have little resemblance to the echo of Barbizon glow in Clague's work and evoke instead the twilight spirit of German Romanticism.

Marshall J. Smith, Jr. (1854-1923)
Manchac Cabin, 1874
oil on canvas
12 x 18 inches
Roger Houston Ogden Collection, New Orleans

Marshall J. Smith, Jr. (1854-1923)
Cypress Grove, Gulf Coast, circa 1880
oil on canvas
16 3/4 x 29 inches
Roger Houston Ogden Collection, New Orleans

Cypress Grove, Gulf Coast is one of the most impressive examples of Smith's personal style, created with the fresh energy of his European experience and applied to the landscape to which he returned. In this work Smith demonstrates a newly acquired ability to depict accurately atmospheric change. The view down a long alley of cypress trees is lit with a soft russet background. The trees have the familiar small brushstroke that Smith came to favor, and which is a distinct technical departure in the Louisiana canon as he employs it. The pinkish cast in the glowing sky enhances the deft use of vanishing perspective. Smith is not content merely to imitate Clague at this juncture or to paint on a grand allegorical scale like Meeker. His compositions become far more naturalistic than Meeker's while retaining the realist agenda laid down by Clague.

The minute brushstrokes which Smith uses in his work help give many of the scenes of ruined farms and desolate fishermen's shanties a rickety feel. Smith's bayou farms are not the lush and productive plantations of the old South order. They are the spoiled visions of new South decay, illuminated by an honest brush.

Smith was most productive during the 1870s and early 1880s, when he was not only busy painting but also active in the emerging artist association movement. He frequently exhibited with the Southern Art Union, and taught various classes there. As late as 1881, however, the *Daily Picayune* for November 5 found that "the artist has not yet learned all the delicacy and finish of which his brush is capable...." During the late years of the same decade Smith slowly abandoned painting to participate in his family's business, a decline that continued until his move across the lake to Covington, in 1906, after which he seems to have painted and exhibited very little. He was a founding member of the Krewe of Proteus and devoted much of his energies to the tableaux and floats of Carnival.

William Henry Buck, Smith's contemporary, began his career with the same indebtedness to Clague. Technically and visually he does not move beyond that precedent, although he did develop a unique personal style. Buck was a Norwegian-born immigrant who began to study with Clague while still working in a cotton-factoring office.

He began exhibiting his work in 1877, and by 1878 was sufficiently successful to garner the praise of the New Orleans *Daily Democrat,* which cited a "most excellent example of Mr. Buck's manner of treating the live oak, the peculiar glory of our Louisiana landscape." Buck often makes the live oak the entire visual focus of his paintings, hung with dripping moss and set against a chromolithographic vision of sunset. Even when his works are fully realized, devoid of suggestive light, these trees appear like implicit essays on the harmony of the landscape.

The newspaper account indicates the semiological importance which the live oak had taken on in the vocabulary of the popular consciousness. This preoccupation is unmatched in any other school of American art. Walt Whitman's poetic description of a live oak in Louisiana growing becomes an extended metaphor for contemplation upon the nature of isolation. "All alone stood it and the moss hung down from the branches,/ Without any companion it grew there uttering joyous leaves of dark green."

Certain newspaper accounts note that Buck was a copiest as well. The chromolithographic quality of his depictions of natural light has much more in common with the spirit of the popular print in the era, the works of Currier and Ives, for example, or the Louis O. Prang Company. These flooded the country with a sentimental image of the old South even into the late nineteenth century.

Buck's masterpiece, and the largest work by him discovered to date, is a painting which demonstrates a far greater degree of compositional originality than any other of his works. *Louisiana Pastoral: Bayou Bridge* is a work where the traditional use of vanishing perspective is abandoned in favor of pictorial realism, concentrating on a humble cabin shanty in a remote bayou. The large overarching tree, the diminutive figures, and the subtle handling of light all echo certain Barbizon trends combined with a sincere regard for a local scene.

With Buck's premature death in 1888, the currents of Louisiana landscape painting turn from the mainstream innovations of artists like Clague, Smith, and Buck towards the more formulaic approaches of a far more academic generation. E. B. D. Julio, whose role as

William Henry Buck (born Norway, 1840-88)
Farm Scene: Bayou Teche, 1879
oil on canvas
16 1/2 x 26 inches
Private Collection, New Orleans

William Henry Buck (born Norway, 1840-88)
Louisiana Pastoral: Bayou Bridge, circa 1880
oil on canvas
26 x 40 inches
Roger Houston Ogden Collection, New Orleans

an instigator of the academic art movement in New Orleans will be discussed later, produced a number of landscapes that were essentially variations on the theme of moody sunsets in distant perspective. G. D. Coulon, that master mimic, does paint brilliant and evocative sunset scenes, but again in the manner of popular prints. In most of his landscapes he re-employs the format of moss-hung trees set amidst pink and green atmospherics. His best work, a large rendering of a scene on Bayou Beauregard, is far more accomplished than any other landscape he undertook, a most satisfying expression of the tones of the foliage set against the reflections in the water.

George David Coulon (born France, 1822-1904)
Bayou Beauregard, St. Bernard Parish, 1887
oil on canvas
24 x 33 inches
Roger Houston Ogden Collection, New Orleans

Harold Rudolph (circa 1850-83/84)
Bayou Sunset
oil on canvas
25 x 30 inches
New Orleans Museum of Art, Bequest of Eugene Lacoste, 15.92

The most melodramatic of these landscape painters was Harold Rudolph, a tragic figure who lived the archetypical life of the starving artist in the French Quarter. Rudolph did master the glowing orange sunset with considerable skill. In these works there is truly the light of Louisiana, at its most extraordinary. Brooding sunsets, set behind the predictable live oak or cypress, lend his works a spirit that is at once luminist in observation and tonalist in feel.

Against this symbolic twilight two creative figures remain to be seen. One, Charles Giroux, is a remote, almost unidentifiable painter whose works have a transcendent quality reminiscent of the New England artist Fitz Hugh Lane. By contrast, the other is so well known that the vast familiarity the public feels for his work has tended, especially in recent years, to cloud his reputation as a genuinely innovative technical and visual composer.

A number of mysteries attend the life and art of Charles Giroux. His place of birth and nationality are as uncertain as his life and tenure in New Orleans. While there is a substantial body of work in his familiar style few are signed or dated, and most have been authenticated on the basis of his unique coloration and compositional conventions. Compounding the mystery of his identity is the

Charles Giroux (born France, circa 1828)
Cotton Plantation, 1850-65
oil on canvas
22 x 36 inches
Museum of Fine Arts, Boston, M. and M. Karolik Collection, 47.1144

Charles Giroux (born France, circa 1828)
By the Bayou, Rural Louisiana Landscape, circa 1860
oil on canvas
14 x 23 inches
Roger Houston Ogden Collection, New Orleans

frequent claim that he was the "teacher" of Blanche Blanchard, a rather celebrated amateur painter and society hostess of the late nineteenth and early twentieth centuries.

Giroux last appears in any known public directory in 1885, when Blanchard was nineteen. While it is possible she had instruction from him as an adolescent, it is unlikely considering that she was away at school in Baltimore during most of that period and she lived in Washington, D.C., during the first Cleveland administration (1884-88). Blanchard did possess several works by the artist, as may be seen in at least one contemporary photograph of her home. It seems quite likely that she added the figures of small animals and fowl to several of his works, then cavalierly inserted her own signature, giving rise to a rather spurious legend that she was his collaborator.

The existence of at least one work dated 1868 seems to mark the first years of Giroux's career.[18] After that date he is listed as a cotton broker in various city directories between 1872 and 1881. In 1882 and 1883 he is listed as "Charles Giroux, painter." He does appear on the roll of the Artist's Association in 1885.

One publication relates Giroux to Richard Clague and John Genin, and labels his painting as "French Beaux Arts." Close examination indicates that Giroux's style resembles the work of neither of those painters, neither of whose art resembles the other's in the first place. Clague's palette, as we have seen, tends toward the muddy tonal colors of the French Barbizon school, heightened by a spare, but direct, light.

Giroux's palette is much more romantic, resembling trends in Berlin and New York state far more than Paris. Furthermore, he applied his paint very evenly, and in a fairly thin layer. This is unlike Clague as well. Genin has a brighter palette than Clague, but a minute brushstroke and photographic quality which renders many of his works flat and derivative.

As to any "Beaux Arts" application of paint, that is most misleading. Certainly early French academic style encouraged the artist to render a highly finished surface, virtually devoid of impasto. However, this was long passé before Giroux's earliest work appears.

That even his contemporaries recognized the special quality of his finished surfaces is recognized in a notice on his work in the October 25, 1885 *Daily Picayune*: "The work is remarkably well finished. The same careful study and painstaking care that characterizes all Mr. Giroux's works is apparent in every line and shadow." Mentioned in that article as well is Giroux's fascination with creating landscapes with an extensive use of vanishing perspective, for a strong sense of depth.

Whoever he may have been, and whatever sources he brought to bear upon his works, quickly fades in importance when one is confronted with the magical qualities of his work. Most have a wonderfully developed sense of light. Frequently he creates a highly romantic tonal contrast between earth and sky, highlighted at transitional periods of the day: dusk and dawn. The smooth register of his coloration, especially the strong blues and dreamy soft peach and pink colors, are quite unique in the canon of Louisiana landscape art.

While he does have a formulaic approach, it rarely seems to be holding his canvas hostage. There is, as well, a sensitive and delicate rendering of the foliage of trees, particularly the cypress, slightly attenuated and discreetly hung with moss. Giroux is neither a scientifically inclined luminist observing the changing patterns of light, nor a somber, nostalgic tonalist. But his is an elusive and captivating figure.

At the end of this long line of moss-hung and sunset-lit landscape artists is Alexander John Drysdale. Drysdale was the last major Louisiana painter to work in the bayou school in a style that continued to evoke symbolic conventions. He attained a position of mythic exaltation during his own life in New Orleans, a position attended by controversy and rumor. Balancing the unsubstantiated claim that his life was one of drunken desperation is a record of

Alexander John Drysdale (1870-1934)
Bayou Scene, 1916
oil on canvas
43 1/2 x 82 5/8 inches
Private Collection, New Orleans

considerable discipline and painterly compulsion, as he is thought to have painted as many as 10,000 works in his lifetime.[19]

Drysdale was the son of an Episcopalian rector, Alexander Drysdale, who served in several churches in Georgia and Alabama before moving to New Orleans in 1883. Once there the young artist received instruction at the Art Union, absorbing the vaguely French techniques being taught by Molinary, Poincy, and Perelli. From 1889 to 1901 he worked as a bank teller, painting at night and staging local exhibitions.

A small legacy he received in 1901 enabled Drysdale to travel to New York, where he studied at the celebrated Art Student's League. While there, he painted with Charles Courtney Curran, Bryson Burroughs, and F. V. duMond, acquiring the best instruction possible in this country at that time. It was at this point that his palette shifted from the bituminous tones of the Louisiana school to a more American Impressionist approach.

In 1903 Drysdale returned to New Orleans and opened a studio at 504 Magazine Street, where he remained until 1920. It was during this period that he made those technical innovations and compositional formats which characterize so much of his work. For subject matter the artist very clearly relied upon the natural scenery in City Park in New Orleans, where he was often seen sketching and painting.

The bayous, water lilies, and live oaks laden with moss that appear in almost all his work were to be seen there in abundance. His work is rarely site-specific despite many attributions of Bayou Teche scenes to him. He tended to use naturalistic elements again and again, using a well-defined, though constantly evolving, visual vocabulary.

The basic Drysdale formula consisted of placing a live oak just to the left or right of the vanishing perspective point on the horizontal bar of the picture plane. The sense of depth was compounded by a stream meandering from foreground to distant background. Overall mood was achieved by the use of a highly tonal blue/grey/green palette—dilute, resonant, and without a strong central light source. Often a soft flowing light from a distant moon or dim sun is to be seen through his celebrated haze, a truly atmospheric grasp of Louisiana humidity.

Drysdale's paint is his most curious invention. He diluted oil paint with kerosene, rendering it very fluid. This medium was then applied to the surface of the work with brush and cotton balls, almost as though it was watercolor with a very resinous compound of gum arabic. This resulted in a work which had a very lush and liquid feel, very much like a fully realized English watercolor heightened with a thin varnish wash.

As long as this medium was being applied to canvas, or to academy board with a prepared surface, there was no problem.

However, Drysdale often used raw paper or a porous type, and these works have shown, with the passing of time, a kerosene ring. Nevertheless, there is a certain appeal in the glowing ring, leached out onto the negative space of the unpainted paper.

After 1920 Drysdale kept a studio in the French Quarter on Exchange Alley. This passage, cut through between Conti and Bienville for access to the St. Louis Hotel, was full of barrooms and street types, and may account for some of the wilder stories about the artist's life.

It may be that Drysdale's substantial output has had an adverse effect on his reputation. There is no doubt that while his formula for landscape composition is somewhat repetitive, each individual work can have tremendous appeal. There is a subliminal calm in many of his works reinforced by the serenity of an overall light source that is neither too strong nor too direct. His sense of color is also subtle and superb, balancing the pleasing harmonies of blue and green. While he may be considered an impressionist, it would be far more perceptive to see him as a late Southern symbolist painter, using the themes of the Louisiana countryside as a motif for his soothing vision of the land of the live oak.

Will Ousley (1866/70-1953)
West Fork of Calcasieu, 1929
oil on canvas
20 x 36 inches
Roger Houston Ogden Collection, New Orleans

Louisiana landscape art hardly ends with Drysdale's death in 1934. But by that time the tides of modernism had begun to overwhelm traditional art in Louisiana, and he appeared out of step indeed. But his achievement, and the achievements of all those painters working in the 100-year period before him, have ensured that the large body of Louisiana landscape art in the romantic atmospheric mode will remain the largest and most intriguing of its type in the entire field of Southern art.

CHAPTER FOUR

Along the River

In any general art historical survey focusing upon painting activity during a limited, and perhaps artificially defined, era, there is a tendency to look for examples of consistent performance. To this point we have looked for examples of portraiture and landscape painting with an eye towards compositional source and conformity to prevailing stylistic trends. However, throughout the history of Louisiana painting there have been artists whose activity was limited to site-specific works illustrating individual events or locales.

Clearly, no other natural phenomenon in the area was as compelling for subject matter or setting as the great river itself. Events affecting the entire course of settlement and development have taken place along its banks. Almost all travel accounts dating from the antebellum period speak of the great variety of spirited settlers beside the Mississippi River. Frederika Bremer, in her volume *America of the Fifties* (November 3, 1850), recalls:

> On the shores of the Great River, exist various scenes and peoples. There are Indians, there are squatters; there are Scandinavians with gentle manners and cheerful songs; there are desperate adventurers, with neither faith nor law, excepting in Mammon and club-law; gamblers, murderers and thieves, who are without conscience and their number and their exploits increase along the banks of the Mississippi the further we progress South.

Not all were bad, as she also found some who were "clear headed, strong and pious men, worthy to be leaders, who know what they are about, and who have laid their strong hand to the work of cultivation." Under these circumstances, it is not surprising that a marvellous, diverse body of art sprang up around these scenes and sagas.

Prior to the rise of a genuine, indigenous landscape tradition in the arts of Louisiana, which, as we have seen, was a relatively late development, depictions of specific sites were limited to the activities of amateurs rendering their homes, or illustrating their travel diaries. One of the first, and certainly one of the best documented examples of an amateurish rendition of a specific locale was painted by Christophe Colomb around 1800. Colomb was a French colonial whose journey to Louisiana may have been induced by the black uprising in Santo Domingo, where he had previously lived. By all accounts he was a lively and entertaining individual who managed to work his way into the affections of Françoise Bringier, the daughter of a wealthy planter, Marius Pons Bringier, of White Hall. Colomb's watercolor of himself seated on the riverbank painting *White Hall* is a whimsical affair juxtaposing flatboats and barges, with a choppy and distinctly foreshortened shoreline. The liberty which Colomb has taken with the breadth of the river at this juncture is forgivable as it permits an excellent view of the distant shore.

Site-specific work was not restricted to plantation views. Historical events, particularly the Louisiana Purchase and the War of 1812, provided additional subject matter incorporating the river vista with the circumstances of battles and statehood proclamations. One early watercolor work, *View of New Orleans Taken from the Plantation of the Marigny* by J. L. Boqueta de Woiseri, was engraved with an important didactic message: "Under my wings everything prospers." Many of the newly enfranchised citizens of the United States of America took note.

Testing the mettle of those new citizens was the War of 1812, a convenient rallying point for political consensus. Jackson's victory in the Battle of New Orleans, in which both the Kentucky long rifle and the pirate fleet of Jean Lafitte were assimilated, had all the right ingredients for popular romance. Capitalizing upon this, the French artist Jean Hyacinthe de Laclotte painted a large and appropriately dramatic view of the battle seen from a great distance, and with sufficient contrast to make an excellent transition to an engraving.

De Laclotte was a French immigrant who seems to have appeared in New Orleans at least as early as 1811. In that year he advertised in the French-speaking newspaper, *La Courrier,* on September 19, 1811, presenting himself as both artist and instructor, in the manner of the day. Together with Mr. Arsens L. Latour he announced a "partnership in the exercise of their profession," an

Jean Hyacinthe de Laclotte (born France, 1765-circa 1828-29, active New Orleans, 1807-15)
Battle of New Orleans, 1815
oil on canvas
29 1/2 x 36 inches
New Orleans Museum of Art, Gift of Edgar William and Bernice Chrysler Garbisch, 65.7

undertaking which would consist of "the building of all public and private edifices...decorations of apartments, gardens, drawings of fancy furniture, and etc." He spent most of his career in New Orleans as a builder and set decorator. Various buildings he designed in the French Quarter and the Faubourg Marigny are extant, and several newspaper accounts of his *grand tableau* appear in the newspapers.

This version of the Battle of New Orleans must have been painted not long after the event itself. When the engraving appeared, the Louisiana *Courrier* for October 27, 1817, reported that the work had "heretofore been seen in this city.... " It was engraved in Paris, and according to the *Courrier,* release of the print was delayed by the "loss of the copy which Mr. Laclotte carried to France." Apparently he sent for the original, which had been left in Philadelphia, and the engraving process ensued.

Once the hostilities with England had been settled and the purchase territory opened to commerce and trade, the lower

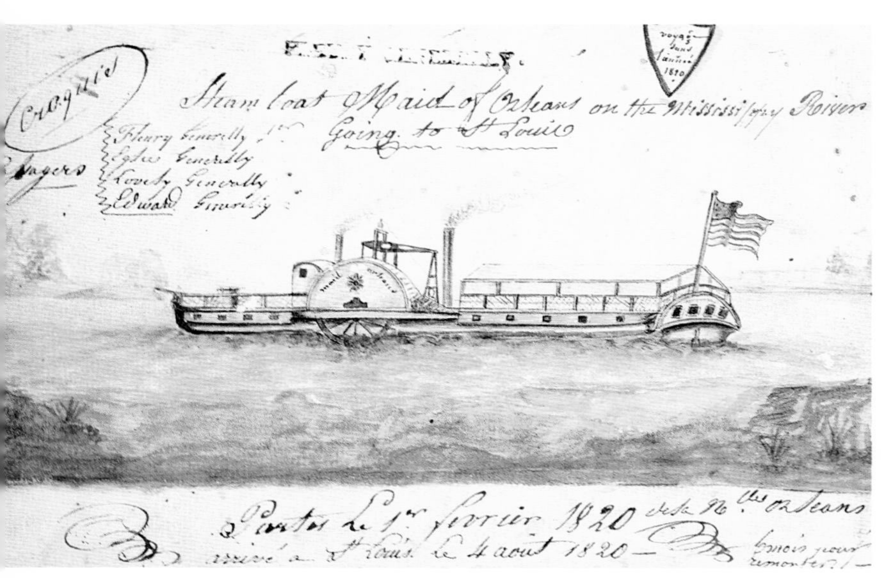

Fleury Generally (born France, 1779-1849)
Steamboat Maid of Orleans, 1820
watercolor on paper
5 1/8 x 8 inches
Tulane University Art Collection, New Orleans

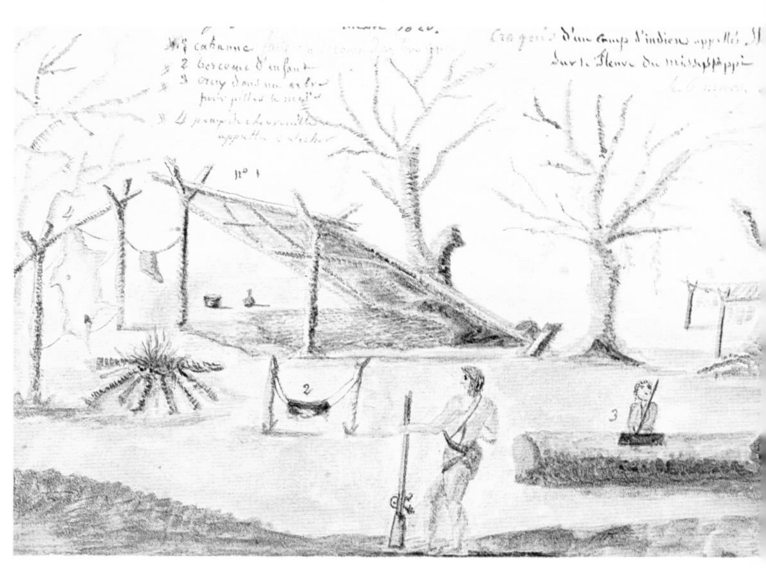

Fleury Generally (born France, 1779-1849)
Indian Encampment on the Mississippi, 1820
watercolor on paper
5 1/8 x 8 inches
Tulane University Art Collection, New Orleans

Mississippi Valley was teeming with boats and settlers and explorers. During the decade of the 1820s Audubon made his downriver trip in search of specimens, painting birds in New Orleans and at Oakley Plantation outside St. Francisville, Louisiana. In 1820 a sign painter of limited abilities, Fleury Generally, made an excursion from New Orleans to St. Louis and painted several watercolor scenes of sites along the way. Generally was French, managed to escape the revolution in both France and Santo Domingo, and worked as both an artist and bookkeeper. His watercolors, while rather flat, do offer a form of documentation on the empty country upriver from the city.

Though not a professional artist, John H. B. Latrobe, son of the distinguished architect Benjamin Latrobe, had a keen eye for detail. His artistic interests had been developed during a period of study with his father, and in the civil engineering discipline at the United States Military Academy at West Point. Latrobe was no stranger to Louisiana. The senior Latrobe worked there in the late 1810s, indeed died there from the yellow fever in 1820.

John H. B. Latrobe married a young woman from an old Mississippi family, Charlotte Virginia Claiborne. In 1834 they determined to spend the winter in Natchez, and travelled to New Orleans, by sea, from Baltimore. Not only did Latrobe keep a journal of that trip, but made watercolor sketches as well.

One of those sketches is a perspectival view, *On the Mississippi, Below New Orleans*. Latrobe was on board an early steam vessel, which was not dependent on wind for power the way more outdated ships were. His picture shows that the "river is filled with shipping which trust to the wind to carry them up. As there is very little of this indispensable commodity stirring today, we have passed everything that we have seen—"[1]

Much that he saw in the area impressed him, for "among the many plantations that I have passed... I have not seen one which did not exhibit the appearance of thriving industry." Latrobe's enthusiasm is tempered by the "melancholy recollection however that the many were labouring for the one in the very worst form of servitude—negro slavery." Latrobe was an ardent abolitionist and early supporter of the state of Liberia.

Black slaves were not the only nonwhites present along the river. Despite massive dispersal and death from disease, substantial

John H. B. Latrobe (1803-91)
On the Mississippi, Below New Orleans, circa 1834
watercolor on paper
7 13/16 x 10 13/16 inches
The Historic New Orleans Collection, 1973.39

François Bernard (born France, circa 1812, active New Orleans, circa 1856-75)
Choctaw Village near the Tchefuncte, circa 1860
oil on canvas
48 1/2 x 34 1/2 inches
The Peabody Museum of Archaeology and Ethnology, Cambridge, Massachusetts

Alfred L. Boisseau (born France, 1823-1901)
Louisiana Indians Walking Along a Bayou, 1847
oil on canvas
24 x 40 inches
New Orleans Museum of Art, Gift of William E. Groves, 56.34

remnants of the native North American population remained in various camps and settlements throughout the upper Mississippi region of Louisiana. Small settlements of these dispossessed individuals were painted by two artists much better known for their portrait activity.

François Bernard, the French portrait artist best known for his large-scale plantation canvases of the establishment, painted one extraordinary work, *Choctaw Village near the Tchefuncte*. Considering the range of Bernard's artistic activity in Louisiana before 1860, this work would seem to date from that period. Neither history painting, nor genre work, the painting is instead a rather curiously didactic historical document. The decay of the settlement is apparent in the condition of the collapsing vernacular log cabins. In the foreground a group of Choctaw women are cooking over an open fire with a rather large bunch of cane before them. A Choctaw man on the right appears to be drinking from an upturned bottle. Squalor and decay is offset by the splendid natural environment.

Alfred Boisseau's painting of *Louisiana Indians Walking Along a Bayou* has no similar narrative implication. Motion in the picture, from right to left, has a theatrical quality, as though the Indians were walking across a stage front. Indeed the compositional format is a reminder of the arrival of the age of photography, which tended to influence the designs of many painters.

Prosperity, especially during the decade of the 1850s, was a great spur to steamboat travel and portage on the Mississippi. The immediate antebellum period was one of unrivaled growth for the city of New Orleans: "Steamboats visiting it from fifty different shores,—possessing the immediate agriculture of its own state, the richest in America and as rich as any in the world...."[2] In the midst of all this activity the port at New Orleans became the most important in the South, and the city attracted a wide variety of international artists, drawn to the scene by opportunity, and subject matter.

One group of steamboats, tied up on the levee in the pool of the Crescent City, seems like an illustration from Twain's *Life on the Mississippi*. *The Belle Creole at New Orleans* evokes the spirit of excitement Twain describes:

> It was always the custom for the boats to leave New Orleans between four and five o'clock in the afternoon.... Two or three miles of mates were commanding and swearing with more than the usual emphasis; countless processions of freight barrels and boxes were spinning athwart the levee and flying aboard the stage-planks; belated passengers dodging and skipping....[3]

In keeping with Twain's observations that "every out-ward bound boat had its flag flying at the jack-staff, and sometimes a duplicate on the verge staff astern," the *Belle Creole* and the *Music* have run

Unidentified Artist
The Belle Creole at New Orleans, circa 1845-49
oil on canvas
48 x 72 inches
The Corcoran Gallery of Art, Washington, D.C., Gift of the Estate of Mrs. Emily Crane Chadbourne

up their colors. Even the perspective is in step with the usual literary theme, for the view is downriver behind the boats.

All of this vibrant activity inspired numerous paintings, drawings, and prints based on the lore of the steamboat. It was a scenario few could resist, "depicting the white wooden swan of a steamboat, gliding along the smooth surface of the Mississippi, gulping superheated energy into her innards, ejecting them hissfully in plumes of white clouds; while overhead soared the flame-tipped, jet-black columns of spent fuel, all moving coincidentally with polished cabins and plush carpet, gay laughter, and clinking chips...."[4]

Events on board also inspired artistic enterprise. William Aiken Walker, best known for his genre paintings, created at least one work which captures the journeyman spirit of riverboat gambling. His card players have nothing of the dash of the riverboat gambler of mythic renown, appearing instead as jolly boatmen of the type painted by George Caleb Bingham. Here, instead of dancing topside, they are hunched over their cards waiting for a lucky break.

William Aiken Walker (1838-1921)
Poker Game on a Riverboat, 1880
oil on cardboard
7 x 10 inches
The Collection of Jay P. Altmayer, Mobile, Alabama

William Aiken Walker (1838-1921)
The Levee at New Orleans, 1883
oil on canvas
19 1/2 x 29 1/2 inches
J. Cornelius Rathbone III Collection, New Orleans

Adrien Persac (born France, circa 1822/1824-73)
Interior of the Steamboat Princess, 1861
gouache and collage on paper
17 x 22 15/16 inches
Anglo-American Art Museum, Louisiana State University, Baton Rouge, Gift of Mamie Persac Lusk

Steamboat interiors could often be as grand as a hotel on land. These floating palaces were several stories tall and could accommodate several hundred people in great luxury. Adrien Persac's *Interior of the Steamboat Princess* has a vanishing perspective point extending deep into the picture plane, enhancing the viewer's perception of the vastness of the dining room.

Persac is one of the more unusual artists to paint the river traffic and scenes in the years before the war. He was a native of Lyons, France, who appears in Louisiana in the early 1850s. He worked primarily as a lithographer and architectural illustrator, as well as map maker. His design for a map of the Mississippi River delineating all the plantations between Natchez and New Orleans was widely distributed in the years immediately preceding the Civil War.[5]

In keeping with his architectural interests Persac also rendered various notarial works used for real estate transactions. His most unusual achievement as an artist, however, was the series of works he painted between 1860 and 1861 of various plantations along the river. These were carefully drawn in minute scale, with the structure often occupying a plane deep within the picture. These works were peopled with figures cut from the popular magazines of the day applied directly to the surface, in the manner of a modern collage. Almost startlingly unique, they have the look and feel of a flat architectural drawing enlivened by a heightened coloration and made amusing by the curious groups of gentlemen, ladies, and workers drawn from the likes of *Harper's Illustrated Weekly* and *Godey's Ladies' Book.*

Adrien Persac (born France, circa 1822/1824-73)
St. John Plantation, 1861
gouache and collage on paper
22 5/8 x 27 3/8 inches
Anglo-American Art Museum, Louisiana State University, Baton Rouge, Gift of the Friends of the Museum and Mrs. Ben Hamilton in memory of her mother, Mrs. Tela Meier

Edward Everard Arnold (born Germany, circa 1816/1828-66)
Battle of Port Hudson on the Mississippi, 1864
oil on canvas
30 x 40 inches
Anglo-American Art Museum, Louisiana State University, Baton Rouge, Gift of the Friends of the Museum

Luis Graner (born Spain, 1867-1929)
New Orleans Twilight
oil on canvas
24 x 30 inches
L. Simon Nelson Collection, Baton Rouge, Louisiana

Alfred L. Boisseau (born France, 1823-1901)
Flood on the Mississippi, 1896
oil on canvas
36 1/4 x 52 inches
The Collection of Jay P. Altmayer, Mobile, Alabama

Not all the river scenes were placid evocations of the romance and power of the river traffic and the grandeur of the stately homes that lined the banks. Late in his career, after he had settled in Cleveland, Ohio, Alfred Boisseau returned to the subject of the river. His frightening image of the Mississippi in full flood is painted with the vigor of high Victorian regard for the power of nature. *Flood on the Mississippi* offers a rather terrifying spectacle of families stranded on the tops of houses, behind the broken levees, and awaiting the arrival of help in the form of rowboat relief squads. Boisseau's painting illustrates one of the most horrific floods in the history of the river. Writing of this flood as a correspondent for the New Orleans *Times-Democrat* of March 29, 1882, Mark Twain calmly observed that one does not appreciate the sight of earth until he has experienced a flood.

The era of river painting would experience substantial transformation with the end of the nineteenth century. Like much subject matter, the river scenes began to be vehicles for stylistic expression, rather than elements of a narrative history of commercial growth and development. Subsequent artists in both the art association movements of the 1880s and 1890s would attempt to portray the river, as would the first generation of Southern impressionist artists working in New Orleans. But the old spirit of place was disguised in avant-garde brushstroke, and like the steamboat itself, slowly faded from the scene, replaced by more modern views.

CHAPTER FIVE

The Black Image in Louisiana Painting

INEVITABLY, AS WITH ANY study that seeks to define cultural patterns in the South, the issue of slavery and race relations emerges as a subject for critical concern. Social and political historians have an easier time, in many respects, dealing with the implications of this issue. Statistical analysis of the existence of slavery is a matter of determining simple figures, much as the history of discrimination lends itself to certain economic and political realities.

Extensive work by historians has created a record that has served to increase understanding in a complex area, enlightening the work of the literary critic and the social reformer. However, very little of that information has been brought to bear on the visual history in the same period. In no other aspect of the history of Louisiana painting does the very nature of the medium provide such extended metaphoric significance.

The earliest depictions of blacks in Louisiana are rather formal portraits, presented in a dignified and straightforward manner. Such portraits were probably always of free persons of color, a separate and prosperous class which flourished in Louisiana as nowhere else in the American South. The creation and development of the Louisiana colony under the French and Spanish "replicated the social experience of the mixed racial systems of the Western Hemisphere, and particularly the French West Indies."[1] By the time

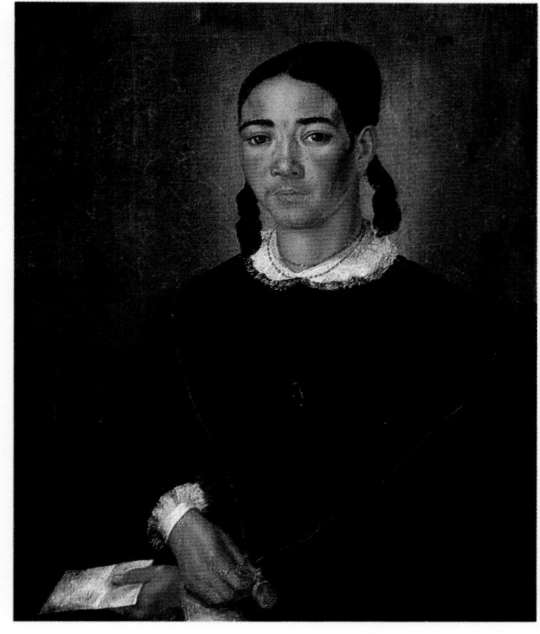

Unidentified Artist
Portrait of a Free Woman of Color, circa 1830-35
oil on canvas
26 x 21 inches
New Orleans Museum of Art, Gift of William E. Groves, 66.29

of the transfer of Louisiana to the United States, there was a large community of free persons of color, financially successful and independent.

The most impressive of these portraits of *gens de couleur libres* is the full-length portrait of Nicholas Augustin Metoyer (1768-1856) by the French itinerant painter, J. F. Fuille, painted in 1836. It shows the wealthy landowner from the Cane River country near Natchitoches pointing with pride to the Church of St. Augustine for which he donated the land. A portrait of a free woman of color, by an unknown artist, also painted in the mid-1830s, depicts a genteel young woman, reflecting the group consciousness of a highly developed social class.

While in the free colored class of the antebellum period there were many sophisticated and accomplished writers and musicians, there were few known visual artists. Among painters, Jules Lion is by far the best documented. Lion was born in France in 1810, where he received his artistic training and exhibited in the Salon. He was active in New Orleans from 1837 until his death in 1866. Besides his portraits of prominent Louisianians, both painted and lithographed, Lion is credited with introducing the new photographic process to New Orleans in 1840, which he probably learned directly from the French inventor, Louis J. M. Daguerre. From his surviving works, it appears that Lion's clientele was drawn from the white establishment, since no portrait of a free person of color by him remains. Among other black painters working in the nineteenth century are Julien Hudson, known only by one surviving portrait, and Alexander Pickhil, from whom no works survive.[2]

Painting is by definition two-dimensional, and all too frequently the restrictions and simple symbolic qualities of the picture plane seem to lend it a hidden agenda of prejudice. Many of the political demagogues of the late nineteenth century rose to power and remained there by creating a fear of black domination over white culture. This "threat" was expounded in harsh oratory, and illustrated with cruel, demeaning prints which rendered the black figure in ludicrously debased terms, a figure of humiliation and simplistic allegory. Throughout much of the period with which we are dealing, the hidden agenda of many white artists dealt with this imagined threat. White supremacy, wrote Ulrich Bonnel Phillips in 1898, "whether expressed with the frenzy of a demagogue or maintained with a patrician's quietude, is the cardinal test of a Southerner and the central theme of Southern history."[3]

The mythic regard which popular culture has come to hold for artistic creation, and the ambiguous quality of genre painting, has only served to compound the problem of interpreting Southern genre paintings that contain black figures. Genre painting is, by definition, a scene of humble life depicting ordinary individuals at their most basic daily tasks. The concerns and implications of genre painting are compounded in the case of the black image, for the visual record created is often a reminder of grave social injustice laden with semiotic import.

Semiotics is the study of signs and messages in language and the visual arts. Just as a painting of a mother and child can convey a message of religious significance to an informed audience, so can a painting of a black field hand convey a message about the basic existence of the rural labor force in the South. From this perspective, the thematic pattern of the black presence in Louisiana genre painting closely follows certain prevailing social ideologies. In the antebellum period, painters viewed the blacks with the same condescending affection for their life and customs that one finds in much of the popular fiction of the period. As in the writings of Harriet Beecher Stowe, a fondness for a group of individuals perceived as simpleminded victims with appealing customs of religion and family becomes a theme in many genre paintings.

One of the best, and earliest, works depicting black folk customs in Louisiana was painted in 1860 by the artist John Antrobus. Antrobus had established a studio in New Orleans in 1859 where he planned to paint a series of twelve large works representing a panoramic view of Southern life. He completed at least two, of which *A Plantation Burial* is the most significant survivor. Within that work a collection of faces, evoking the vocabular arrangements of a baroque morality painting, conveys attitudes from despair to boredom. So clearly is the focus upon the activities of the slaves, that the master and the mistress are only remote figures, hidden in the shadows of the trees on the left, mute spectators to a pageant of religion and personal expressions of grief.

Religion offered a profound emotional outlet for the black slave, serving also as a tool of passive resistance to the order imposed by the master. Eugene Genovese, the distinguished social historian, has carefully read various slave narratives for evidence of cultural consistency with existing patterns of black African culture:

> A slave funeral became a pageant, a major event, a community effort at once solemn and spirited. The slaves preferred to have a service, but they would not readily do so without a display. In this way they carried on West African tradition, according to which a proper funeral would put the departed spirit to rest and would guarantee against the return of a stirring ghost—a view held by some rural blacks in the twentieth century. Funerals thus served as a conduit for the departed's entrance into the spirit world.[4]

Within the canon of extant works from the antebellum period, little of the violence and oppression of the later era is foreshadowed in the pieces depicting black slaves at work, in harmony with the

John Antrobus (born England, 1831-1907)
A Plantation Burial
oil on canvas
52 3/4 x 81 5/16 inches
The Historic New Orleans Collection, 1960.46

existing social order and full of domestic virtue and devotion. François Bernard, the society portraitist, painted a work in which a mulatto woman offers her baby to a Sister of Charity, a scene as rife with melodrama as little Eva's passage to Heaven in *Uncle Tom's Cabin*.

Following the war, however, a new approach to black subject matter emerged, one that depicted the harsh realities of rural black life in Louisiana. Of those artists who used the black as subject matter in this period, the best known is William Aiken Walker. Walker is, in many respects, one of the most familiar artists to a larger audience of painting in the region, as his works were often engraved and sold as colorful chromolithographs.[5] He was also a staple of the tourist souvenir trade, and legends about him are more enduring than those surrounding any other painter who ever worked in Louisiana.

Walker was actually born in Charleston, South Carolina, and spent at least part of his youth in Baltimore, Maryland. He began to paint while still a child, and pursued some formal studies in

Baltimore at the Maryland Institute both before and after the outbreak of the war in 1861. He did enlist in the Confederate Army, and served four years in the Southern theatre.

Following the war, Walker began a pattern of seasonal itinerancy much like that of an antebellum portraitist. However, he did not paint portraits, but rather small souvenir-sized paintings of rural black life. He made his first appearance in New Orleans in 1876, returning to the city almost every winter until 1905.

During his stay in New Orleans, Walker painted two types of genre works with black subject matter. The first type has the look and feel of certain French works in the Barbizon mood. These paintings have a naturalistic style which accurately details the landscape, plantation architecture, and black laborers objectively presented in the context of their worklife.

Comin' from the Market near Baton Rouge is a careful, well-accomplished work which may be viewed as a visual document of Reconstruction and the restoration of the Louisiana agrarian economy. In much the same way, Walker's many cabin paintings,

William Aiken Walker (1838-1921)
Comin' from the Market near Baton Rouge
oil on canvas
14 x 20 inches
The David Warner Foundation, Tuscaloosa, Alabama

William Aiken Walker (1838-1921)
Cabin Scene, 1883
oil on panel
6 1/8 x 12 1/4 inches
New Orleans Museum of Art, Gift of Mr. and Mrs. Edward C. Henderson, 70.3

such as *Cabin Scene* in the collection of the New Orleans Museum of Art, offer a documentation of vernacular building type. With their different chimneys and swept yard arrangement they do indeed create an important visual record. However, vernacular architecture was not Walker's only concern. For what we see in the art of William Aiken Walker, and several of his contemporaries, is the hidden agenda of racial prejudice.

The second type of work Walker painted was far more harsh than pleasant scenes of rural agrarian labor. At the time of the Cotton Exposition in 1883, Walker painted several works with the caption "Whar am dat Expersision?" which showed an elderly black couple—lost, seemingly ignorant, and dressed in deplorable rags—wandering through the wharves on the river in search of directions. Nothing in the presentation of blacks in these works in any way reflects their basic humanity, potential for growth, or status as free men and women.

While these images now seem remote, condescending, and discriminatory, they served a specific social function. By creating a lens through which the disparate elements of two cultures bound together in paternalism and strife could be seen at some level of emotional, and economic, interdependence, the art of the period sought to create an organic unity of form. That form called for the acceptance of certain economic, social, and racial roles which are now as archaic as the static figures in early Greek art. But they were widely embraced in the period in which they were created, one of the greater ironies of the visual arts.

Developments in the use of black figures in the visual arts had international impact as well. In the minds of many American and European painters working in the late nineteenth century, images of the rural laborer came to be identified with the flight from the savage inhumanity of the industrial state. As experienced in the art of certain French Barbizon painters, these humble workers become the first antiheroes, epitomizing the virtues of rural life.

Rural workers standing in a field and contemplating the rising or the setting sun as they went about their work came to be the standard fare of popular prints. Two of Walker's best-known paintings, *The Levee at New Orleans* and *A Cotton Plantation on the Mississippi,* were reproduced by Currier & Ives in 1884. The latter even came to be used as an advertisement for cotton swabs. Both these works are constructed with compositional devices and stock figures which Walker liked to repeat.

Unlike most of his contemporaries, Walker does not use a traditional vanishing perspective point to suggest depth and heighten the narrative qualities of his work. Rather, he places his figures in parallel planes, front to back, locking them into a gridlike system which emphasizes their hostage situation. The appearance of a steamboat, or gin, or wagon in the front enhances the visual variety of the planes, otherwise only broken up by the anonymous teams of workers.

The message of Walker's large *Where Canal Meets the Levee* is quite clear. Reconstruction is over, the cotton economy is booming, and things have returned to normal. The white planter and white businessman who stand in the center congratulating themselves on the prosperity they see around them are segregated from the black figures who sit idle, dressed in rags, and staring stupidly out of the picture plane. Such works of art contributed to the stereotypes of blacks which persisted until quite recently.

Walker began painting in Louisiana during the worst, and most violent, days of political reconstruction, which followed the end of the war in 1865. In Louisiana, the situation was so bad that in 1874 an armed revolt against the black militia was staged in New Orleans, with considerable loss of life and damage to property. The harmless, idyllic peasantry of genre paintings was also the despised, newly enfranchised class seeking political and social integration.

The unrest of the Reconstruction period coincided with the rise of the academic art movement in New Orleans. Andreas Molinary was among the most prominent artists in that movement. In 1876 he painted a work of a black prisoner that is one of the most subliminally unsettling works created in the period. Bound, strapped

William Aiken Walker (1838-1921)
Where Canal Meets the Levee
oil on academy board
12 x 10 1/4 inches
Robert M. Hicklin, Jr., Inc., Spartanburg, South Carolina

Andreas Molinary (born Gibraltar, 1847-1915)
Prisoner, 1876
oil on millboard
12 x 9 inches
L. Simon Nelson Collection, Baton Rouge, Louisiana

to a chair, and unable to see, the figure is being held hostage to the same frightening mentality represented by the author of *Carpet-Bag Misrule in Louisiana.* Within that article white supremacist ideology is endorsed as a "wise, stable, and practical government."[6]

Far more violent emotions were present in the same age, resulting in literary and artistic expressions springing from an agenda which was hardly hidden. Throughout the Reconstruction period (1866-76), public protests were mounted to the government of the "carpetbagger," a term of "reproach [which] referred to those who were exploiting the negro in politics and depriving the Southern people of their birthright," according to one contemporary account. One of Walker's contemporaries, George Henry Clements, has left behind a group of letters and articles which sharply document the more horrific aspects of the racist agenda of many of these genre painters.

Clements was a native of Louisiana, born in New Orleans. His family also had a plantation near Opelousas. Inspired by the visual and intellectual possibilities of the local scene, Clements pursued a career as an artist by painting portraits in his spare time, when not busy as a clerk on the Cotton Exchange. By 1880 he took formal instruction in New York, and moved to that city where he remained for seven years. In the summer of 1887 Clements returned to New Orleans, painting there and on the plantation at Opelousas. Several letters which he wrote to his dealer, J. Eastman Chase, are extant. Within those letters Clements does little to disguise his true feeling about the local scene, describing the life at hand in terms which hardly match the Victorian prose he would subsequently place in print on the same subject:

> Have been on the old plantation a week now...am delighted with everything, even the fleas. There are no mosquitoes & the country is divinely beautiful & it isn't horribly hot at all. Lots of dogs & cows & niggers to paint—everything primitive and innocent, except myself.

Clements' coarse assessment of the scene and individuals at the plantation is a jolting reminder of deplorable conditions and attitudes which were to continue well into this century and which still exist in many areas.

However, when he came to write of the same locale for an article which appeared in the August 1887 *Arts and Letters,* his description suddenly becomes more philosophic:

> I was astonished and delighted beyond expression by the superlative beauty and vitality of our Delta landscape. The colossal oaks, magnolias and rank weeds half concealing old mansions, sugar houses, and cabins: gleaming groups of negroes (and negresses...the Southern peasantry) delving and singing in the green fields and cattle browsing in pastures bounded by cypress swamps. These, with the swan like steamboats on

> the broad Mississippi, present a group of picturesque details unique and valuable to all lovers of the beautiful—above all to those who live for and by it.

The divergence in mood between Clements' two expressions of interest, one coarse and racist and the other high-minded in a Victorian manner, characterizes the artist's work. *Sharpening the Knives* seems harmless enough until the monotony of the work, and the depressing circumstances of the surrounding world, are fully realized. At that point, the divergence between the idyllic pastoral worker and the oppressed minority becomes apparent.

While works of the type painted by William Aiken Walker, George Henry Clements, and Andreas Molinary continued to dominate the genre painting scene until the Second World War, there were artists who saw other possibilities in black culture. E. B. D. Julio, who figured prominently as a founder of the academic art movement in New Orleans, painted at least one work, *Har Yar,* which evoked more of the true Barbizon spirit of idyllic rural life than racist manifesto. In keeping with the transition in artistic styles which characterizes the first years of the twentieth century, there is, as well, a shift in the uses of subject matter. So much of late-nineteenth-century Louisiana art in the Barbizon mood is a pale reflection of a major European trend, a reflection made even weaker by the application of that style to works that are far more illustrative than pictorial.

Visiting artists to Louisiana during this period seem to be compelled to use local scenery and black subjects in an allegorical manner. F. Arthur Callendar, for example, was a Boston painter who spent the year 1892-93 teaching at Tulane while painting a series of works to be displayed in the Louisiana pavilion at the Chicago World's Fair. A small study for one of these works survives, *New Orleans from Algiers,* a painting that combines many of the most familiar elements from Louisiana landscape and genre painting. There is the levee road, the winding river, the vernacular cabin, and the black woman, encumbered with a load of wash on her head and attired in the kerchief and turban of the working class.

New Orleans artists working in the impressionist manner in the early years of this century painted the black subject in far more sympathetic terms. Many of these artists discovered that the black condition and anatomical form lent itself to a heroic image, a persistent classical theme in Western world art. At the same time a rich black culture was emerging around the city, particularly in the jazz music of the French Quarter.

During the years which followed the First World War, a Northern artist, Wayman Adams, spent most of his winters in the French Quarter painting portraits, and making drawings for a series of lithographs. Adams had studied with Robert Henri and William

George Henry Clements (circa 1855-1935)
Sharpening the Knives, 1881
oil on canvas
14 1/2 x 17 1/2 inches
Roger Houston Ogden Collection, New Orleans

F. Arthur Callendar (born Boston, died after 1917, active
New Orleans, 1892-93)
New Orleans from Algiers, 1893
oil on canvas
15 x 24 inches
Roger Houston Ogden Collection, New Orleans

Wayman Adams (1883-1959)
New Orleans Mammy, circa 1920
oil on canvas
50 x 40 inches
Southeastern Newspaper Corporation Collection on loan to the
Morris Museum of Art, Augusta, Georgia

Merritt Chase. Like his contemporaries Clarence Millet and Helen Turner, he brought the rich palette and textural variety of the American impressionist movement to his Louisiana subject matter.

One of the largest works which he painted in this period is a portrait called *New Orleans Mammy.* While the subject herself is a familiar type, the manner in which she is painted marks a radical departure in the depiction of black subjects. Here, the painterly qualities of the surface of the work add intense interest to the folds of the clothing, the background detail, and the presence of the sitter. Adams' work is a celebration of the visual potential of the subject rather than an illustration of condescension.

Toward the end of the period under study, one of the most important artists to paint the black experience began to work and exhibit in New Orleans. John McCrady was the son of an Episcopal minister and spent his youth in the rich rural folk cultures of Louisiana and Mississippi.[7] From 1930 to 1933 he studied at the University of Mississippi, and in various studio programs in Philadelphia and New Orleans.

John McCrady (1911-68)
Portrait of a Negro, 1933
oil on canvas
21 x 17 inches
Roger Houston Ogden Collection, New Orleans

McCrady began to take classes at the New Orleans Art School in 1932, an organization sponsored by the Arts and Crafts Club, an outgrowth of the old New Orleans art associations. While there he painted *Portrait of a Negro,* which he submitted to the annual scholarship competition sponsored by the Art Students' League of New York. He subsequently won a one-year scholarship for further study in New York.

Portrait of a Negro marks a new beginning for the uses of black subject matter in Louisiana art. For the first time, the naturalistic potential of the person is fully explored, and some element of dignity and individual personality is revealed in the work. It is an essay on facial features, anatomical form, and the play of light and shadow in a very minimal setting. A work of tremendous subtle presence, it clearly impressed the judges.

While McCrady was in New York he was exposed to the teachings of Thomas Hart Benton, and the art of the American regionalists. American art during the 1930s took a divergent path from European abstraction, returning, in the midst of the great economic depression, to the history and pictorial traditions of this country. Artists like Benton, Grant Wood, and John Steuart Curry painted the customs of their native regions with an appreciative eye, tempered by occasional subtle caricatures of the more extreme affectations of provincial life.

Once McCrady finished his year and returned to Louisiana, he began to paint the myths and realities of his own local scene with the same depth of perception he had seen in the other regionalist artists. McCrady often chose to paint both black and white subjects. His *The Shooting of Huey Long,* which will be discussed in the chapter on the modern movement, has the same strong narrative content as many of his works focusing upon the black community.

McCrady's first great national success came in 1937, when his work *Swing Low, Sweet Chariot* was exhibited in New York to widespread acclaim. The New York *Herald* found that "Mr. McCrady combines fantasy and realism with a quiet humor in his work...." While the painting is a simple allegory, it has a much greater appeal than the works of artists like William Aiken Walker. The work suggests a universal parable of death and salvation hardly restricted to the world of the black. As in Antrobus's work from the earlier

John McCrady (1911-68)
Swing Low, Sweet Chariot, 1937
oil on canvas
37 x 50 1/4 inches
The St. Louis Art Museum, Eliza McMillan Fund

century, it is a painting which records a folk custom, imaginatively conjuring up the eternal struggle between good and evil for the soul.

After the painting was shown in New York, McCrady returned to New Orleans and a much greater recognition for his work. For the next ten years he continued to pursue the theme of black religious life, inspired, at least in part, by his tremendous interest in black gospel music:

> The music that surrounded me all my young life, and which was as natural to my environment as any other element of nature, was that which I experienced in the songs that came from the Negro, an expression of a religious philosophy crossed with the legends and myths that would startle and alarm, a philosophy acquired from the white man combined with a metaphysical heritage from the darkness of Africa....

However deep McCrady's appreciation may have been of black culture, he worked in an era in which major shifts in the perception of social interaction guaranteed that he operated from a narrow precipice. In 1946, the *Daily Worker* of the Communist Party in America denounced his paintings as flagrant examples of racial chauvinism, a charge to which he was most sensitive. After that time McCrady did not return to rural black religious life as subject matter.

Unlike William Aiken Walker, who has left behind no letters or recorded conversations which define his goal as an artist, McCrady commented at length on his goals:

> I see in painting one way of expressing our age, the people and their surroundings, their philosophy of life, the emotional reason for their being—as well as my own destiny to thus interpret the meaning of life, as I see it, to those people who are my neighbors.

McCrady's interpretations, together with those of a small group of his fellow artists, helped to herald a new day in the modern era's depiction of the black subject. Alberta Collier's finely realized studio work of a mulatto woman is a sophisticated academic statement. Marion Souchon, an accomplished and talented self-taught artist working in the mid-century, painted several black musicians with verve and an abstract perception.

Alberta Collier (1911-85)
Mulatto Woman, 1938
oil on canvas
34 x 24 inches
Roger Houston Ogden Collection, New Orleans

Towards the end of the period under consideration a black artist emerges, one whose naive but genuine depictions of black plantation life offer a contrast to the works of William Aiken Walker and other white artists. Clementine Hunter was born around 1886 on Hidden Hill Plantation near Cloutierville, Louisiana, but while an adolescent her family moved to Melrose Plantation in the Cane River country. Melrose was the site of Cammie and John Hampton

Henry's historic preservation efforts which have been affectionately recorded by Lyle Saxon in his book, *Old Louisiana*. The Henrys attracted many New Orleans artists and writers to Melrose, and one of these, Alberta Kinsey, seems to have unwittingly inspired Hunter when she left behind some paints after a visit in 1940.[8]

Clementine Hunter (1886/87-1988)
Flowers Always Make Friends, circa 1940
oil on paper
13 x 11 inches
Yvonne Ryan Collection, New Orleans

Hunter approached François Mignon, curator at Melrose, with a desire to use these remnants to "mark" a picture of her own. From that point she painted with great energy, producing several thousand works in a certain formula, all representing black rural life. She began exhibiting in 1949 and soon gained the reputation as Louisiana's black Grandma Moses.

As with works of many self-taught painters, there is a flatness and absence of clear anatomical detail that somehow works as a deeply personal expression. Most often the figures in Hunter's paintings are shown at work, in profile, and in bright primary colors. They are characterized by an appealing childlike naiveté, a gentleness which relieves the monotony of repeated compositions. Most importantly, they are indigenous visions, unaffected by a longing for financial gain, or fame as a purveyor of tourist commodities.

Throughout this period in the history of painting, objects were created that have black subject matter but which are not specifically black in any extended cultural context. What is most amazing about the transformations which occur in the history of the black image in Louisiana painting is the heroic status the black figure will come to embody in the late twentieth century.

CHAPTER SIX

Academic Art Associations of the Late Nineteenth Century

WITH THE ADVENT OF the Civil War and the rise of photography as a popular medium for taking portrait likenesses, the art of Louisiana experienced a great sea change. Both events lessened the demand for portraiture, and the itinerant portrait artist disappeared from the Louisiana scene as a compelling messenger of taste. Portraiture did linger on as an art form, but after 1865 it became, more than ever, restricted to a monied class seeking status. Diminished demand also meant that fewer artists from a broad range of ability came to live and work for periods of time in the state.

Those artists who were left after the war began to pursue other art forms. As we have seen, it was during the challenging days of Reconstruction, from 1865 to 1875, that a true Louisiana style of landscape art emerged from the traditions of Richard Clague. Indeed, while art activity immediately following the war was sporadic, it was a time that proved particularly productive for several of the indigenous Louisiana artists who had painted in the state and returned there from Confederate service to live and work.

In an effort to renew interest in the agricultural economy of the state, several agricultural and mechanical fairs were held between 1866 and 1870. At several of these Richard Clague won prizes for his landscapes, prizes which would help finance his artistic pursuits. These fairs, which were loosely based on the success of the Crystal Palace exhibition in London in 1851, also encouraged interest in art activity, and paved the way for a genuine academic tradition in the late nineteenth century.

Theodore Sidney Moise (1808-85) and Victor Pierson
(active New Orleans, circa 1865-73)
Life on the Metairie, 1868
oil on canvas
56 x 72 inches
The Fairgrounds, New Orleans

Undoubtedly the most remarkable work to be produced during the period and shown at the fair in 1868 was Theodore Sidney Moise's and Victor Pierson's *Life on the Metairie,* a gigantic work depicting several well-known figures in the racing world. Moise had enlisted in the Confederate Army and served throughout the war, rising to the rank of major with the forces of General Hebert. Upon his return to New Orleans he seems to have resumed his old pattern of forming partnerships with other artists, as his collaboration with Pierson on the Metairie racetrack picture would indicate.

Victor Pierson was an English artist about whom very little is recorded other than various listings in directories and newspaper advertisements for his services as a portraitist. He may have shared Moise's enthusiasm for animal painting, for the self-portrait of him which survives is a genre work of himself and Moise riding together in a buggy being drawn by two horses and chased by a large dog. Moise sits upright and appears very cavalier in a summer suit as he drives the buggy. Pierson, looking every bit the part of the English gentleman, sits on the other side in a proper bowler hat; mustachioed and holding a cane. In terms of size and compositional

Victor Pierson (active New Orleans, circa 1865-73)
T. S. Moise and Victor Pierson in Buggy, circa 1872
oil on canvas
34 1/2 x 42 1/2 inches
Louisiana State Museum, 579

Victor Pierson (active New Orleans, circa 1865-73) and Paul Poincy (1833-1909)
Volunteer Firemen's Parade, 1872
oil on canvas
72 x 108 inches
Louisiana State Museum, 7881

detail, it is really one of the more ambitious works from the immediate postwar period.

Paul Poincy (1833-1909)
Our Lady of Lourdes, 1874
oil on canvas
66 1/4 x 50 inches
L. Simon Nelson Collection, Baton Rouge

Large ambitious group portraits or historical works seem to have been the order of the day. In 1872 Pierson collaborated with Paul Poincy on another rather remarkable group portrait, the depiction of the firemen's brigade assembling for their parade on March 4, 1872, and gathered around the statue of Henry Clay. Both artists are reported as working on that painting in the August 17, 1872 New Orleans *Bee,* which also notes they have "on exhibition...a remarkable portrait of Horace Greeley, candidate for the United States Presidency."

Like many of his contemporaries, Poincy was another artist who was also a Confederate veteran. A native New Orleanian born of French aristocratic emigres, he had been educated by the Jesuits in New Orleans prior to six years of study in France at the Ecole des Beaux Arts. His apprenticeship in the studio of the academic master Julien may have planted the seed of naturalism which flowers in his mature work.

According to the New Orleans *Bee,* Poincy and Pierson had access to panoramic photographs of the firemen's parade taken by Theodore Lilienthal, a photographer and art dealer who had a studio on Poydras Street in the central business district. Lilienthal also sold photographic reproductions of the painting. As we have already seen in the concluding days of antebellum art, photography was becoming increasingly important as a historical record, displacing portraiture as a means of preserving the likeness of a beloved family member. But with the sure knowledge that Pierson and Poincy used photographs to paint the firemen's parade, the implications of photographic sources take on a far more significant cultural note.

Strains of naturalism and realism apparent in the landscape art of the period did little to disguise the poverty of the land after the war. Those same strains are also present in the quest for accuracy in several large group portraits. This is not just a manifestation of certain ongoing nineteenth-century concepts of "truth" in art, but reflects the emergence of a genuine tradition in style. An accurate likeness and an honest representation of the scene replaced more romantic mood compositions.

Furthermore, the collective nature of the subject matter is also of great importance. Throughout the 1870s, there was an increase in large, all-male organizations. It was during this time that the major Carnival krewes took on the importance that they have sustained to the present. At the same time, secret societies were also formed to repress blacks. Group portraiture served to augment the hidden agenda of male bonding and white supremacy.

Writing of the first days of extended Carnival celebration, the visiting author Edward King notes that the "krewe of Comus has

Paul Poincy (1833-1909)
Dogs in the French Market, 1889
oil on canvas
44 x 50 inches
New Orleans Museum of Art, 25.0

Paul Poincy (1833-1909)
Still Life with Radishes, 1906
oil on canvas
10 3/4 x 13 13/16 inches
The Historic New Orleans Collection, 1966.9

always paid the expenses of these displays itself, and has issued invitations only to as many people as could be accommodated within the walls of the theatre to witness the tableaux."[1] From the beginning these krewes would prove to be an essential source of income for several important academic artists, including Andreas Molinary and Bror Wikstrom.

Accurate likeness, gigantism in history painting, and the formation of artistic societies may all be seen as coming together in a single artwork and in the life of the artist Everett B. D. Julio.[2] Julio was a native of the island of St. Helena in the South Atlantic. He made his way to this country before the war, and studied for a time at the Lowell Academy in Boston under the visionary painter/sculptor William Rimmer.

Everett B. D. Julio (born St. Helena, 1843-79)
The Last Meeting of Lee & Jackson, 1869
oil on canvas
108 x 72 inches
Robert M. Hicklin, Jr., Inc., Spartanburg, South Carolina

During the war years, Julio, whose Southern sympathies were quite pronounced, moved to St. Louis, where he could be near the cause of the Confederacy without suffering the fate of illegal aliens behind the lines. While he was living in St. Louis, he conceived of a great scheme to create a series of monumental paintings of Southern military leaders in action. The first version of *The Last Meeting of Lee & Jackson* was actually painted in St. Louis.

This work, which became the icon of the "lost cause" movement in the late-nineteenth-century South, is an imaginary scene based on the final meeting between Generals Lee and Jackson on the evening of May 2, 1863, prior to the battle of Chancellorsville. That battle would prove to be Lee's last substantial victory and would result in Jackson's death. With all of those metaphoric ingredients involved in the historical composition, plus the enduring appeal and emerging cult of Lee, it is little wonder that the work attracted considerable attention when it was first exhibited in New Orleans on January 20, 1870.

Julio, though an artist of enormous ambition and some talent, had very little money; he struggled through the end of the decade like the quintessential starving artist. After having offered the work to General Lee, who declined the honor, he felt inspired by Lee's remarks on the likenesses, and the spirit of the picture, "to look forward to a glorious future, as I felt, through proper study I could proclaim myself the historical painter of the South, towards which goal I am now struggling...." Like Pierson and Poincy, Julio had used various photographic images of Lee and Jackson circulating in popular journals as a source for his painting. But unlike them he was new to a city in the grips of an economic depression and had few resources other than his artistic vision to support himself. The lotteries and auctions he attempted to stage to sell the work also proved unsuccessful in the economic climate. Even a print of it, which sold quite well throughout the South, made little money for Julio, whose poor business acumen resulted in his being duped for the copyright.

Last Meeting was on almost constant display in New Orleans from 1870 to 1879, most often in Julio's studio or in the Wagner Art Gallery on Camp Street. At first Julio survived on the proceeds of the exhibition, painted a few portraits and genre works, and entered the arena of Louisiana landscape art. Feeling that he lacked sufficient training to pursue his art, he determined to return to Europe for further education in France. To achieve that goal he painted a copy of *Last Meeting* for Colonel David French Boyd, the president of Louisiana State University, who paid him $1,000, a sum adequate to finance his trip abroad.

Once in France, Julio had a great dream, that of creating a large academy for teaching art in New Orleans. Writing to President Boyd he notes that he is collecting plaster casts for future "antique" drawing classes he would like to offer when he returns, for "there is nothing so improving to the youth as a knowledge of drawing and it is my hope to be able to do something of the sort in New Orleans." When he returned to New Orleans he took up residence at 8 Carondelet Street, across Canal Street in the American district, but within a short distance of the French Quarter and the St. Charles Hotel, a central meeting point. He painted, arranged exhibitions of his work and the works of other artists (including Richard Clague), and did indeed teach, though perhaps not on the grand scale he had imagined.

Many of the works which Julio exhibited in his studio/gallery were of an avant-garde nature, painted in the style of the first generation of impressionist art. In announcing the display of such works, Julio expresses himself in the popular press with his usual bravado:

> In this collection there are a number of simple effect and color studies, which represent certain facts; these should not be looked upon as daubs, but accepted...as any connoisseur would, as a color, or natural study effect.

Through this combination of salesmanship and teaching, Julio managed to survive and prosper, though only for a while. In 1879 he died from tuberculosis in Georgia, where he had gone to escape the stifling climate of New Orleans. William Aiken Walker may have been at his bedside, and he was genuinely mourned by his contemporaries in the art world.[3] While the New Orleans *Times* was not exactly flattering concerning either his talents or his aspirations, it did publish this note in his obituary:

> [Julio] conceived the grand idea of establishing in this city a school of design.... He pictured to himself an art school of large and scientific proportions...he soon found, however, that the scheme was in advance of the age in which New Orleans now lives....

George David Coulon (born France, 1822-1904)
Spirit of Louisiana, 1884
oil on canvas
45 x 27 inches
New Orleans Museum of Art, Gift of the Fine Arts Club of New Orleans on the occasion of their sixtieth anniversary, 76.69

John Genin (born France, 1830-95)
Spirit of Louisiana, 1884
oil on canvas
44 x 22 inches
The Collection of Jay P. Altmayer, Mobile, Alabama

The scheme was not all that much in advance, as it turns out, for after Julio's death his studio was taken over by the painter Andreas Molinary. Within the next year, Molinary and a group of other artists, including George David Coulon, William Henry Buck, Marshall J. Smith, Jr., and Paul Poincy, would form the Southern Art Union and offer the first organized classes in art instruction in the area.

On May 4, 1880 the New Orleans *Bee* announced that it had "received a synopsis of an organization now being formed under the title 'Southern Art Union' the object of which is to place in contact all persons, residing in our city or in the Southern States, who cultivate the fine arts either by profession or as amateurs." Although art instruction and commercial distribution were clearly the intent of the school, the preamble of the charter, adopted at a meeting held in the Ladies' Parlour of the St. Charles Hotel on May 26, 1880, is full of high-blown ideals: "The object of this society is to promote the culture of all aesthetic tastes—to collect works of art—to encourage artists—and generally to foster and extend those high and purifying influences which the love and pursuit of art engender." By choosing to meet in the Ladies' Parlour of the most elegant hotel in the city, the society gave a clear indication of which arena it hoped to draw support from.

As early as November 1881, the School of Art of the Southern Art Union, listing its address as 203 Canal Street, offered "the services of a distinguished watercolorist" who would "teach painting on porcelain." While the arts profession remained a male-dominated field, "china painting" was a genteel occupation for young ladies and one which was likely to increase membership in the classes to the profit of the school. Within the same announcement, the presence of a Miss Tuzo is noted, and in January 1882, the School could offer "lessons in china painting and painting on silk and satin" given by her. A brief note on the availability of instruction in "Kensington Art—Needle Work" is an indication of the first stirrings

John Genin (born France, 1830-95)
Surf Bathing, Grand Isle, circa 1870
oil on canvas
10 x 36 inches
New Orleans Museum of Art, Gift of Sam Friedberg, 52.42

John Genin (born France, 1830-95)
Pontchartrain Beach, circa 1870
oil on canvas
10 x 36 inches
New Orleans Museum of Art, Gift of Sam Friedberg, 52.43

August Norieri (1860-98)
Three Sailboats
oil on board
12 x 18 inches
New Orleans Museum of Art, Ella West Freeman Foundation
Matching Fund, 71.13

of the arts and crafts movement in New Orleans, as well as other developments under the Woodward brothers.

Achille Perelli, the sculptor and watercolorist, had charge of the first drawing classes the Union offered, which were announced in a series of articles in the local papers beginning in January of 1882. A reporter, visiting these classes, notes that his students were occupied with making "drawings from the flat, that is copies of other drawings, and copies from casts and sculpture, chiefly heads from the Antique." The same reporter also notes that he has also seen "copies of landscape in pencil and sepia" as well as "some well executed drawings of architecture and machinery by pupils of Col. L. J. Fremaux's class in...geometrical and engineering delineation."[4]

The climate of taste into which the Southern Art Union was born was one in which the appreciation of art was a rather obscure pursuit. As one artist anonymously confided to a newspaper reporter in 1881, "We have to restrict our subjects to certain styles to suit popular taste, and a portrait painting is the only kind of work that is remunerative." While this had been the traditional lament of artists in this country since Benjamin West's initial ambitions to be a history painter in 1760, the next remark the nameless source makes is much more specific:

Achille Perelli (born Italy, 1822-91)
Blue Crab and Terrapins, circa 1880
gouache on cardboard
23 3/4 x 15 1/2 inches
New Orleans Museum of Art, Gift of Samuel Weis, 56.90

> An obstacle to be encountered here by any artist who attempts compositions of a higher order is the difficulty of obtaining models. There are not in New Orleans, as in the cities of Europe, persons whose ordinary business it is to serve as models.

Whether from inclination, prudishness, or the lack of models as mentioned, the initial description of classes at the Southern Art Union make no mention of "Life Classes" or drawing from a real model.

The absence of life classes with real models was not restricted to New Orleans, nor does it indicate any greater degree of provincialism concerning the human anatomy than was accepted and practiced in other major American art academies. Throughout the period the standard text for human anatomical study was William Rimmer's *Elements of Design,* a volume which isolated the anatomy into a series of phrenological interpretations based upon the skull shape and size, and which purported to connect character traits with anatomical details. Julio had absorbed these theories during his stay in Boston before the war, and perhaps brought some of them to New Orleans with him. For the health and continuity of the school, the instructors apparently were not especially interested in obtaining nude models; it would hardly have satisfied the parents of their female students.

By comparison, it should be noted that the search for "truth in art" at the same time the academy was opening took on a double meaning. On the one hand, artists like Molinary and Perelli were espousing, and pursuing, the high-minded "art for art's sake" doctrine that the Union's preamble articulates. In other parts of the city and in the nation at large, artists whose concern with pictorial realism amounted to a far more genuine idealism were breaking with convention and attempting to create new academic procedures.

Of these, Thomas Eakins' efforts at the Pennsylvania Academy of Fine Arts are the most historically significant.[5] In the same year in which the Southern Art Union was founded, Eakins began his series of paintings based on the incident of William Rush sculpting his allegorical figure of the Schuykill River using a live model. Eakins' profound admiration for Rush stemmed in part from his own desire to introduce life classes into the curriculum of the PAFA, which he headed at the time. His resignation in 1886 was a response to the Academy's increasing resistance to such innovations, and his subsequent career was a pioneering effort to change American academic standards in the teaching and practice of painting composition.

Notices in the local papers and a healthy enrollment indicate that the Southern Art Union had popular, if not widely diversified, support. A review praising an exhibition of drawings from Perelli's class thought the overall excellence spoke well of "the systematic art instructions organized and set on foot by the managers of the Southern Art Union." The same review goes on to offer a provocative challenge: "There is no reason that New Orleans should not be the center of taste and influence in Art, radiating to other sections of the Country, but so desirable a result can only be obtained by systematic and substantial encouragement and support of the culture of those who are really gifted in that direction."

If only by default, New Orleans was becoming a major art center for the South, the center of the greatest amount of art activity. After more than one hundred years in which there had been thriving art activity, the area was moving towards a stable residential art community. Within that community, a group of artists, largely immigrants from the Mediterranean basin, were helping to shape a specific style of Louisiana art, one which combined certain elements of the ongoing landscape formula with still life and religious objects.

Between the dissolution of the Southern Art Union in 1884 and the formation of the Southern Artist's Association in 1885, the "World's Industrial and Cotton Centennial Exposition" opened. This rather lumbering affair covered some 245 acres and involved the exhibitions of most of the states in the union and several foreign countries—and it was doomed to be a dismal financial failure. Yet the presence of an "Art Building" some "250 feet long by 100 feet wide, furnishing 25,000 feet of floor space, and by its internal dividing walls affording 20,000 feet of wall space," made it a critical art event.

Most of this wall space was taken up by the works of American artists who accounted for 280 of the 900 works hung. Of these, however, very few were Louisiana works, Andreas Molinary, Charles Wellington Boyle, and Achille Perelli being the local artists represented. Other artists represented in the exhibition included Ruger Donaho and Benjamin Constant.

The exhibition would have afforded both the local artists and the local art-viewing public their first substantial encounter with major national and international art movements. One historical account of the exposition notes that the works of Ruger Donaho, a Mississippi native, were "imbued with the teachings of the modern French School." Along with the impressionist works Julio had done, this introduction of elements of French impressionism to the local scene would have profound implications for the generation of artists who emerged during the 1890s.

Much less avant-garde, but no less influential, works by artists like Constant and Chelmonski indicate an ongoing interest in the peasant studies of the Barbizon School, and in Orientalism. Exotic North-African Orientalist scenes begin to appear after this exposition from the brush of several of the Southern Artist's Association members, especially Achille Perelli. The exhibition may have spurred collecting interest as well, for the foundations of the Hyams Collection (a core of the New Orleans Museum of Art) had been established by this time, and many of the works in that collection reflect a similar taste.

William Henry Buck painted the exhibition halls several times, creating frames from intertwined rusticated twigs, meant to give a picturesque setting to the otherwise utilitarian structures. Apparently the Art Building itself was rather unimpressive. Historian Herbert Fairall found that it "conveyed an impression of substantial strength rather than of architectural grace."

Although most of the formal art organizations of the 1880s and 1890s were short-lived, they did provide the first cohesive climate for artistic creation which had existed in the city or state. The principal characteristic of antebellum art activity was itinerancy punctuated by the short-term residential efforts of artists who, while talented, were primarily functioning as theatrical set decorators and only created easel paintings as time allowed. However, after the war, a more diverse—and more settled—community took root.

The diversity of the art community is in many ways a reflection of the diversity in the New Orleans population. Artists from old Creole families like Poincy and Coulon worked with recently arrived painters like Molinary. The arrival of the Woodward brothers in 1884 ensured a fresh current of style in the form of the fledgling arts and crafts movement, tinged with French impressionism.

The coalescence of this community of artists is apparent in the number of organizations, social clubs, and periodic publications. Meetings in the studio of Andreas Molinary in 1879 resulted in the formation of the "Cup and Saucer Club," so named because each member needed to bring his or her own china. These informal social gatherings created an audience and membership for the larger arts organizations of the 1880s.

One of the most substantial changes in the make up of these societies was the presence of women members drawn from the rising numbers of female students and ambitious amateur writers from both the uptown and French Quarter areas. From this group, talents as varied as Mary Townsend and Grace King would emerge.

This contact between the literary and art worlds would soon result in New Orleans' first art periodical. "The cumulative effect of these events was a flowering of the arts," Judith Bonner has written. "The idea of a journal integrating literature with art was conceived to provide a platform and outlet for the groups' collective creative efforts."[6] *Arts and Letters,* which was to consist of six issues published between 1886 and 1887, is the most important document of the cultural climate surrounding the artist's associations. Among those artists who contributed illustrations were Bror Wikstrom, William H. Buck, and Ellsworth Woodward.

Andreas Molinary (born Gibraltar, 1847-1915)
North Shore, Lake Pontchartrain (Fisherman's Cabin), 1881
oil on canvas
24 x 36 inches
Walker Y. Ronaldson, Jr. Collection, New Orleans

It was a time when many, in the words of Grace King, were attempting to "break the shackles that bound New Orleans to a political past that held her in a kind of commercial servitude, with her wheels of progress slowed down to an immobility that threatened to become a permanent condition."[7] With renewed economic prosperity and a vision of Louisiana's historical significance restored, many prominent artists found new sources of patronage as well as peer support.

Of all the academic artists working at this time, the most energetic was undoubtedly Andreas Molinary. Molinary was a painter willing to apply his brush to many subjects. Examples of portraiture, still life, landscape, and nature studies survive.

His landscape work has the essential atmospheric qualities which we have previously identified. His still life work was far more delicate and detailed, and may have been the inspiration for his most dedicated student, Marie Seebold, the daughter of the gallery and art-supply store operator. He was also a teacher in the association's schools, and a frequent judge of local art competitions. In some accounts he is given credit for encouraging Isaac Delgado to establish an art museum in the city.

Molinary survived most of his contemporaries in the Artist's Association, lingering, blind and ill, under the care of Marie Seebold, who had become a very accomplished painter of floral still life

Andreas Molinary (born Gibraltar, 1847-1915)
Old Gentilly Road, 1890
oil on canvas
32 x 48 inches
Roger Houston Ogden Collection, New Orleans

Andreas Molinary (born Gibraltar, 1847-1915)
Still Life with Violets and Roses, 1907
oil on panel
4 x 7 1/2 inches
Roger Houston Ogden Collection, New Orleans

works. She was married to him on his deathbed in 1911. He was buried in Metairie Cemetery. In keeping with his origins on Gibraltar, he stipulated that a "simple boulder, typical of the rock from whence he came," be placed over his grave.

Achille Perelli, Molinary's contemporary, was also an artist who worked in several mediums. He was born in Milan, Italy, and like many other Europeans, fled the continent in the aftermath of the revolutions of 1848. He was a finalist in the competitions for the Jackson Square sculpture in 1851. Perelli is often confused with an artist with a similar name, and similar origins. Achille Peretti (1857/62-1923) was an academic painter who specialized in religious works and church decoration.

Throughout his long career, Perelli alternated between sculpture and painting. His work in the Greenwood Cemetery and the adjacent Metairie Cemetery included busts of notable leaders of the Confederacy, including Robert E. Lee, Stonewall Jackson, and Albert Sidney Johnson. He also executed many private portrait busts.

Perelli was best known for creating a series of startlingly realistic trompe l'oeil images of dead game, hanging from a nail on an imaginary wall in the Dutch still life tradition. A visitor to his studio from the *Daily Picayune* in February 1874 found an "image of a woodcock hanging by its feet to a nail—all so subtly limned that you are at a loss to tell the model from the semblance as they confront you side by side...." Perelli's illusion came complete with "a large blue bottle fly which threatens the purity of Mr. Perelli's sketch," although a closer inspection reveals that "Mr. Perelli created the fly also."

These images of dead game, or *nature-morte,* were a staple of late-nineteenth-century academic painting in New Orleans. Judging from the numbers of them which survive, by artists as far ranging as Perelli, George L. Viavant, and Coulon's son, George Amede Coulon, they were clearly a profitable pursuit, desirable to local sportsmen as trophies and to tourists as empathetic reminders of the lush surroundings of the swamps and bayous of Louisiana. The still life tradition surrounding fish and game was extensive, and well in place prior to the Civil War. William Gerdts and Russell Burke have noted that "at the mid-century there existed a national (one is tempted to say international) school of painters of dead game and fish, who enjoyed popularity and reputations unequaled by any other still-life painters in America up to that time."[8]

In the South, William Aiken Walker painted these types of still life works, based on his studies in Baltimore, before the war. But Perelli was the first artist to establish a reputation for *nature-morte* of works after the war. They are rendered in very accurate detail, and together with Perelli's other paintings of game, living as well as dead, they make, in the words of Gerdts and Burke, "an unusual contribution to the subject matter of American still life painting."

Marie Seebold (1866-1948)
Hat Full of Cherries, 1895
oil on canvas
17 x 21 inches
L. Simon Nelson Collection, Baton Rouge, Louisiana

Achille Peretti (born Italy, 1857/1862-1923)
Head of a Saint, 1897
oil on canvas
29 x 29 inches
L. Simon Nelson Collection, Baton Rouge, Louisiana

Achille Peretti (born Italy, 1857/1862-1923)
Supplication, 1897
oil on canvas
33 1/2 x 25 inches
L. Simon Nelson Collection, Baton Rouge, Louisiana

However, the unquestioned master of the trompe l'oeil still life genre was George L. Viavant. Viavant was a native New Orleanian from a distinguished Creole family. At the age of twelve he enrolled in the Southern Art Union, where he was instructed by Perelli in the techniques of painting and drawing. Perelli taught in the established European manner, providing his students with subjects for anatomy studies, and drilling them in accurate rendering. Viavant worked with Perelli, developing a superb drafting technique from both casts and life, for nine years.

In 1884 he exhibited a work in the Cotton Exposition student competition, and was awarded a blue ribbon. From that point Viavant was actively engaged as an artist in the world of galleries and collectors. In 1889 he moved to the family plantation on Bayou Sauvage, Gentilly. An undated newspaper feature by G. William Nott, now in the collection of the Louisiana State Museum, notes that from this spot "nestled amidst giant magnolias and towering pecan trees, whence is wafted the fragrant perfume of the sweet olive and orange blooms, far from the hurry and bustle of modern New Orleans, the artist naturalist brings forth his master works."

Mention of Viavant as an "artist/naturalist" recalls the career of Audubon. Like earlier artists, Viavant took to the fields and

George L. Viavant (1872-1925)
Duck, 1921
watercolor on paper
25 1/2 x 14 inches
New Orleans Museum of Art, Gift of Carl Biehl, 85.103.6

George L. Viavant (1872-1925)
Wild Turkey
watercolor on paper
54 x 42 inches
Mr. and Mrs. James Viavant, New Orleans

George L. Viavant (1872-1925)
Rabbit, 1913
watercolor on paper
28 x 15 inches
Mr. and Mrs. James Viavant, New Orleans

streams of Louisiana to note the on-site habits and look of a variety of wild game. He tended to work in a larger format than Perelli, and with a very colorful palette. The degree of realism and the vivid coloration give the works a highly finished, sophisticated quality, making them among the most accomplished works of any artist painting in this style at the end of the century.

Viavant was but one of several local artists whose career was nurtured by the organization of the Southern Art Union and its successor organizations. The lists of artists who received instruction there is extensive, including talents as diverse as the gifted amateurs Edward Livingston and Blanche Blanchard, and more accomplished artists like Lulu Saxon and Alexandre Alaux. Saxon created at least one monumental view of Magazine Street admirable for scale and handling of depth and perspective. Alaux was successful as a miniaturist, a painter of local scenes, and as a historical muralist in the older traditions of the nineteenth century.

Much of what is known about the history of art in Louisiana up to this time is the result of documentary efforts made by the artist Bror Wikstrom. Wikstrom arrived in New Orleans in 1883 following a stint as a merchant marine in Scandinavia. He had embarked upon an art career in his native Sweden after several years at sea and received his most serious training at the Royal Academy of Fine Arts in Sweden.

Alexandre Alaux (born France, 1851-1932)
Avondale Ferry, circa 1900
oil on canvas
28 x 40 1/2 inches
J. Ray Samuel Collection, New Orleans

Lulu King Saxon (1855-1927)
Uptown Street, 1890
oil on canvas
90 x 68 inches
Roger Houston Ogden Collection, New Orleans

Wikstrom's interests and pursuits were many and varied, in keeping with the eclectic nature of the classic studio artist. He was a founding member of the Artist's Association, subsequently serving as corresponding secretary and president. He also taught sketching in the Association's classes.

Wikstrom's most visionary achievement was his sponsorship of the periodical *Arts and Letters,* which we have noted as the most important journal of its day. Though far less glamorous than his art activities, Wikstrom's contributions as an interviewer and scrapbook keeper are critical. From the evidence present in scrapbook no. 100 at the Louisiana State Museum, it would seem that Wikstrom kept clippings, interviewed artists, and made notes on objects from the founding of *Arts and Letters* until his death in 1909.

It was Wikstrom who encouraged Coulon, the oldest living artist of his day, to write down his memoirs and recollections of earlier Louisiana painters. These represent the only substantial primary material in the entire period. Wikstrom himself was an accomplished painter prone to re-creations of marine scenes from his days in the Scandinavian fjords. He painted a few portraits and at least two impressive Louisiana landscapes composed in the full vocabulary of the genre.

There is no doubt that he made his living primarily as a Carnival designer, executing elaborate sets for the Rex and Proteus pageants. Surviving sketches of these works reveal them as ambitious scenarios with the same pomp one sees in the first silent movies. Wikstrom was sought out by several cities to help with fairs and pageants. Indeed, while in New York in 1909 to prepare a parade for the Hudson-Fulton celebrations, he took ill and died.

Considering the achievements of the academic painters working in Louisiana during the late nineteenth century is a somewhat antiquarian affair. Many of their images are delightfully fanciful evocations of historical events and local scenes glimpsed through the entirely genteel lens of Gilded-Age New Orleans. It is rather sobering to consider that at the same time artists like Marshall Smith and Bror Wikstrom were creating Carnival sets, Winslow Homer, John Singer Sargent, and Thomas Eakins were bringing more painterly, and more intellectually charged, revolutions to American art. While there are important strains of tonalism and a naturalistic concern for both environment and individuals present in many of the Louisiana landscape works in the period, there is little evidence of profound originality. What is important about the organization of the various artists' associations is the climate of interest in art they created, and the important access to genuinely professional instruction they offered.

Alexandre Alaux (born France, 1851-1932)
Evangeline
oil on canvas
80 x 83 inches
Louisiana State Museum

Bror Anders Wikstrom (born Sweden, 1854-1909)
Fishing in the Swamp, 1886
oil on canvas
36 x 54 inches
Yvonne Le Mercier du Quesnay Collection, New Orleans

By stimulating the market and providing both instruction and gallery outlets, the organizations paved the way for far more original, indigenous artists in the twentieth century. Even as they existed, the Woodward Brothers were bringing the arts and crafts revolution to New Orleans. Many early-twentieth-century painters received their first lessons from these quaint old masters. Their work now has the same quality their contemporary George Washington Cable found in the Vieux Carré. For like that old Quarter, it is an art where "beauty lingers...to say nothing of the picturesque, sometimes you get a sight of comfort, sometimes of opulence...a glimpse...of much similar rich antiquity."[9]

CHAPTER SEVEN

The Woodward Brothers: Reflections upon Art and Manufacture

During the final decades of the nineteenth century, the Romantic paranoia that had induced many artists and writers to disparage the onset of the industrial revolution subsided. The fantasy landscapes and dreamy poetry of that generation gave way to the thoughts and actions of the arts and crafts movement, a movement which sought to incorporate the best thinking on the value of making art into the creation of art associations and, even more importantly, schools. Above all other concerns, practical usage ranked as the highest priority, as the gospel of "art for art's sake" was considered decadent.

In England this movement had been given even greater impetus by the royal family. Under Prince Albert's auspices, and with the proceeds from the Crystal Palace Exhibition of 1851, the Kensington consortium of art and industrial institutions was created. These museums and schools, based on certain German examples, became the models for blending usefulness and creativity, fulfilling William Morris's and John Ruskin's hopes that through art the world could be made a better place. "I cannot forget," Morris once said to an important gathering in Birmingham, England, "that...it is not possible to disassociate art from morality, politics and religion."[1]

Deep in the Southland, on the campus of the faltering University of Louisiana in New Orleans, it seems that a faint echo of that sentiment was heard. Paul Tulane, discouraged in his efforts to give some of his vast fortune to Princeton University, had instead found a welcome home at the University of Louisiana, and provided

William Woodward (1859-1939)
French Market, 1904
oil crayon drawing on black composition board
22 x 28 inches
New Orleans Museum of Art, Gift of Stern Family Fund, 61.41

the means to reorganize that institution, subsequently renamed in his honor. From the beginning of the reorganization, President William Preston Johnson felt that excellence in the manual instruction of art was imperative. When Johnson asked William Woodward to come south and teach at the newly formed Tulane University, he set in motion the Louisiana arts and crafts movement.

Together with his brother, Ellsworth Woodward, William was to create a substantial body of art which drew upon the landscape and architecture of Louisiana. Important as that art would prove to be in terms of inspiration for preservation and creativity, the thought and example of the Woodward brothers was even more significant. Through their lives and work, Louisiana art finally left the wandering world of the itinerant, and came to rest in an aesthetic which combined the local spirit with the priorities of truly international art movements.

Both William and Ellsworth Woodward were eminently trained and suited to the roles which they were about to occupy in the cultural life of Louisiana. They came from a New England family with strong traditions of teaching and founding libraries. Both had been schooled at the Rhode Island School of Design, an art institution based on the South Kensington model and staffed, at least in part, by English instructors.

William Woodward was asked to come to Tulane in 1884, the same year the Cotton Centennial was affirming a local interest in the arts. When Woodward first came to Tulane he taught in the galleries of the Government and States Building at the fair, which occupied a site in what is now Audubon Park, across St. Charles Avenue from Tulane and Sophie Newcomb College.

After Woodward had been hired by Johnson, he spent the summer of 1886 at the Académie Julien, in Paris. The Académie Julien was at that time one of the foremost centers for the study of academic art, and while there, Woodward absorbed lessons in formal French design and instruction. When he returned to New Orleans later in that year he was made a full professor at Tulane, and pursued courses in what was then called "manual training."

At the same time he offered free evening drawing classes to students pursuing commercial careers, which attracted such a large attendance, especially among young women, that they were later expanded and incorporated into the curriculum of Sophie Newcomb College. William Woodward selected his brother, Ellsworth, to head up the Newcomb School art department.

Ellsworth Woodward (1861-1939)
Paradise Wood
oil on canvas
28 x 40 inches
New Orleans Museum of Art, Purchase by Board of Administrators from Art Association of New Orleans, 29.1

Ellsworth Woodward (1861-1939)
European Village, Germany, 1909
watercolor on paper
15 x 21 1/2 inches
Roger Houston Ogden Collection, New Orleans

Ellsworth Woodward (1861-1939)
Self Portrait, 1889
oil on canvas
18 x 15 inches
L. Simon Nelson Collection, Baton Rouge, Louisiana

Like William, Ellsworth was a product of the Rhode Island School of Design, but unlike his brother, he had pursued further training at the Munich Academy in Germany. This represents a rather fascinating departure, for it means that between them the two brothers had technical training in the two prevailing schools of Western Europe. These different approaches are most apparent in their earliest works in Louisiana when they served as model instructors for art trends found outside the Mediterranean basin instincts of the old academics.

The distinctions between approach to design and coloration are most apparent in this early work. William Woodward always prefers a lighter palette and there is in his work, particularly the oil crayon renderings of the Vieux Carré, the sense of light and shadow which characterizes French impressionist art. Specifically, William Woodward tended to create a sense of mass and form through the use of color, rather than a strong geometric composition through deep contrasts.

Ellsworth Woodward's exposure to the Munich Academy is most apparent in his understanding of light and shadow. His work tends to be more in the spirit of Frank Duveneck and the Cincinnati School of art. This involves a rather heavy shadowing, in which the light emerges from the shadow to create a more somber, tonalist effect.

As is often the case with artists whose careers are lengthy, and whose academic associations are extensive, the Woodward brothers were innovative and challenged the provincialism of the New Orleans art world with currents of ideas circulating in the Northeast and in Europe. Their careers spanned the rise of American impressionism and the cubist revolt of the early twentieth century. In works like Ellsworth Woodward's portrait of his wife, *Mary by Firelight,* there is that startling and altogether satisfactory sense of light emerging from shadow that characterizes so much of the Munich Academy style. At the same time, as we have seen, the Woodwards made peace with the older academic painters of New Orleans, illustrated their periodicals, and eventually included them in the plans for the Isaac Delgado Museum of Art.

Both Woodward brothers are frequently mentioned, in subsequent critical accounts, as Southern impressionist artists. In his introductory remarks for a Tulane exhibition catalog, William Cullison wrote:

> The influence of Impressionism upon the Woodwards is to be seen in the beautiful effects of light and atmosphere which characterize their work generally, and, in oil paintings, in their exuberant brushwork and vibrant colorism.[2]

The Woodwards in turn influenced their Southern contemporaries with this style. Whether the genuinely revolutionary implications of impressionism were realized by the brothers seems a subject for further consideration.

Above all else, impressionism, as it developed in France, represents the most significant change in artistic attitude of the last thousand years. Once the impressionist artist began to create volume and mass on the picture plane by brushstroke instead of a well-honed drafting line, all of art changed from a uniform academic expression to one of individual genius.

The great sea change wrought by French impressionism became most apparent in the years following the first exhibition of such paintings in the Salon des Refusés in 1874, at a time when the Woodwards were still adolescents drafting under the old rules of the Rhode Island School of Design. The appearance of the first impressionist works was truly startling. As Helen Gardner has pointed out, "The fact that at closer range the surfaces of their canvases look unintelligible, and that forms and objects appear only when the eye fuses the strokes at a certain distance accounts for much of the adverse criticism they received...."[3]

However, it is important to note that what was genuinely revolutionary to the overbearing establishment in Europe became something far tamer in America. Here, impressionism was transformed into an expressionistic style filling a vacuum in the world of art. It was in this spirit that the Woodwards learned, and painted.

William Gerdts, the foremost authority on American impressionism, has made this observation:

> The reasons for [impressionism's] early acceptance in this country are many and complex: certainly the lack of a strong academic tradition against which impressionism was a reaction, is important. Also, impressionism took on poetic and decorative overtones, and American impressionism often compromised impressionist tendencies, as well as with more low-keyed tonalist art....[4]

William Woodward (1859-1939)
Back Bay Moon, Biloxi, circa 1920
oil on fabric
11 1/2 x 8 1/2 inches
Roger Houston Ogden Collection, New Orleans

Poetic, decorative overtones do characterize much of the Woodwards' art, especially William's sensitive and ethereal oil sketches of the Mississippi Gulf Coast by moonlight, which dissolve form into vertical bands of light and color reminiscent of Whistler's great works painted in Valparaiso Harbor.

An awareness of impressionism would have come easily to the Woodwards through their continued summer travels to Europe. Ellsworth in particular rendered a number of astonishingly brilliant watercolors of the places he visited there. Impressionism was useful in portraying Louisiana locales, and this is clear in many works painted by the Woodwards in the state. Gradually, the style took root in the South, where it continued to be practiced long after far more avant-garde innovations were born in the Northeast.

The style seems to be in keeping with the Southern sense of place. Rick Stewart has pointed out in his essay on this age in *Painting in the South,* "many Southern...artists of the period had an individual view that began with a highly developed sense of place, including the belief that the artist had to draw his material from his native area in order to achieve spiritual and artistic regeneration."[5] Stewart directs this remark, most appropriately, to the large number of landscape artists working in the impressionist mode in Louisiana, including the Woodward brothers, William Posey Silva, and Alexander John Drysdale. Because the Woodward brothers were also teachers whose students became teachers, many Southern impressionist artists working in the state, including Helen Turner and Clarence Millet, guaranteed that this would be a lasting style in the area.

Donald Keyes' observation that "the accomplishments of long-overlooked Southern-related practitioners of impressionism exemplify the completeness of the style's national triumph"[6] should be affirmed and amplified. Impressionism did take root in the South in the works of a number of native and visiting artists.[7] However, it is an art of genteel impressionism of the most elusive sort, applied to the landscape as a means of illuminating without defiling. Even the Woodwards practiced this. Though they painted such scenes less frequently than landscapes, they too presented dreamy mothers with children in delicate, beautiful settings.

Genteel impressionism is a concept that would be completely in accord with the Southern self-image emerging in the late nineteenth century. Impressionism was the perfect technique to convey a misty world of moonlight and magnolias, the world being fabricated by the generation of postwar Southern writers. Thomas Nelson Page spoke with an apologist voice when he asked if it mattered that the course of the South "has been different from that which the old seers foretold, if the future be somewhat veiled in mist!"[8] Mist is precisely what one looks through in much of Louisiana impressionist landscape art, a mist which both obscured and enhanced.

While William Cullison lauds the Woodwards for their depictions of "the exotic Louisiana-Mississippi Gulf Coast landscape, with its characteristic oak and pine vegetation and heavily liquid atmosphere," he offers certain critiques as well. "Viewed critically, the Woodwards cannot be said to have used the Impressionist idiom in a particularly original or innovative manner," he concludes. While that may be the case, the application of the impressionist style by the Woodwards verifies certain notions of Barbara Novak, whose discussions of style transformations have provided a running theme in this study.

Novak writes most persuasively of the persistence of certain American attitudes, rather than particular academic art forms or styles. In her view, much of American art is a manifestation of a specific, informed approach to subject matter, instead of a wrenching intellectual search for an accepted style. Most relevant for any consideration of the Woodwards' achievements, she points out about Mary Cassatt that she "rarely allow[ed] light and color to disintegrate form."[9]

The Woodwards did not allow this either, even when William was at his most misty in the uses of Raffaelli oil crayon to capture the mood of the old French Quarter. William Woodward had long been interested in architecture, considering it to be an integral part of the plastic arts and vital to the practical curriculum being developed at Tulane University. As early as 1894 he had been appointed a "Professor of Drawing and Architecture" at Tulane. He brought together at the school a group of architects to develop competitions for designing important civic structures, and he was ultimately responsible for the establishment of the Tulane School of Architecture in 1907.

Considering William Woodward's love and appreciation for architecture, it is not surprising that he was greatly alarmed by plans in 1895 to tear down the old Cabildo on Jackson Square. He was, at that time, chairman of the art committee of the Art Association of New Orleans, and as such, was successful in helping to save

William Woodward (1859-1939)
Second Ursulines Convent and Priest's House, 1912
oil crayon on cardboard
22 x 28 inches
New Orleans Museum of Art, Gift of Stern Family Fund, 61.31

the building. Public concern for the historic structures and spirit of the French Quarter eventually culminated in the creation of the Vieux Carré Commission, which even today preserves that part of the city bound by the river, Rampart Street, Canal Street, and Esplanade Avenue.

But this concern had a profound artistic effect as well. In 1895 William Woodward began to paint the structures of the French Quarter on site. Michelle Heidelberg pointed out that, "as he painted *en plein air* setting up on a street corner, in an alley or in the middle of a street, it was hard and messy for him to mix the oils and blend his colors."[10] To cope with that situation, he began to use the Raffaelli solid oil crayon, a stick with a medium that could be applied like pastel, but which had the luminous surface quality of oil.

The crayons were quite effective for on-the-spot use. Brilliantly colored, they captured all the blinding, shimmering light quality of the Quarter on a sunny day, or the moody look of rain on the ancient tiles and rotting plaster. Unfortunately, the binding medium in these crayons has not proven to be stable, and the works are subject to flaking. It was a technique that Woodward pursued for more than twenty years. In the course of that time he created scores of images of the French Quarter, recording structures which have subsequently been destroyed, and inspiring the preservation movement that has secured for posterity the vast majority of extant buildings.

Ellsworth Woodward (1861-1939)
Portrait of William Woodward, circa 1910
oil on canvas
27 1/2 x 19 1/2 inches
New Orleans Museum of Art, Gift of Carl E. Woodward, 61.58

Woodward's constant willingness to participate in a variety of art forms induced him to accept a commission from the United Fruit Company to paint a mural on the ceiling of the lobby of their headquarters on St. Charles Avenue. It was an ambitious project requiring extensive scaffolding. When the mural was nearly complete, Woodward suffered a terrible fall which severely damaged his spine and kept him in a wheelchair for the rest of his life. In the next year he retired from teaching and began to build a studio/ home on the Gulf Coast near Biloxi, Mississippi, keeping his New Orleans connections as well.

For the next eighteen years Woodward continued to paint, travelling extensively throughout the country in a specially equipped car as he searched for new sites. Painting became more difficult as he grew older, and he turned to print making, employing a new technique called fiberloid to engrave his Raffaelli oil sketches of the French Quarter. These were eventually collected into a uniform edition in 1936 and sold for the benefit of the Vieux Carré Commission. After a brief illness, William Woodward died in 1939.

Ellsworth Woodward's career was encumbered by more administrative responsibilities than that of his brother. From 1890 until 1931 Ellsworth was chairman of the art department at Sophie

William Woodward (1859-1939)
Dome of the St. Louis Hotel in the Rain, 1915
oil crayon on cardboard
28 1/4 x 22 1/4 inches
New Orleans Museum of Art, Gift of the Art Association of New Orleans, 60.2

William Woodward (1859-1939)
Royal Street Courtyard, The Court of the Two Sisters, circa 1924
oil crayon on cardboard
29 x 23 inches
New Orleans Museum of Art, Gift of the Stern Family Fund, 61.33

William Woodward (1859-1939)
Biloxi Gulf Coast Scene, 1892
oil on canvas
18 x 30 inches
Mr. and Mrs. Patrick Taylor Collection, New Orleans

William Woodward (1859-1939)
Moon Over Lake Pontchartrain, circa 1920
oil on masonite
7 x 10 inches
Roger Houston Ogden Collection, New Orleans

William Woodward (1859-1939)
Woodward House, Lowerline and Benjamin Streets, 1899
oil on canvas
31 7/8 x 36 5/16 inches
The Historic New Orleans Collection, 1979.376.1

William Woodward (1859-1939)
Oleanders, 1924
oil on canvas
27 1/2 x 21 3/4 inches
Private Collection, New Orleans

William Woodward (1859-1939)
Pass Christian, 1905
oil on canvas
24 1/2 x 39 3/8 inches
Private Collection, New Orleans

Newcomb College, and in that capacity oversaw the activities of the Newcomb School of Pottery. He was also a founder of the Delgado Museum, serving on its board from its inception in 1910 and as volunteer director from 1925 to 1939. He was president of the Art Association of New Orleans and the Southern States Art League. Perhaps his greatest achievement was becoming director of the Works Progress Administration project on art in New Orleans, which collected hundreds of documents on artists and resulted in a fifteen-volume encyclopedia of material largely digested from newspapers.[11]

Ellsworth was capable of painting large oils with a profound appreciation of place. The somber qualities of many of his landscape works are relieved by a strong light playing among the towering pines and murky swamps. One oil in particular, a view of oranges on a tree in his backyard at Covington, is a powerful essay on form—naturalistic form in near chaos, close to the picture plane, strongly colored, and equally strongly composed.

Ellsworth Woodward (1861-1939)
Backyard in Covington
oil on canvas
35 1/2 x 47 1/2 inches
L. Simon Nelson Collection, Baton Rouge, Louisiana

Ellsworth Woodward (1861-1939)
Interior at the Alhambra, 1905
watercolor on paper
21 x 15 inches
Roger Houston Ogden Collection, New Orleans

Ellsworth Woodward (1861-1939)
Bruges, Scene with Goat, circa 1890
watercolor on board
10 3/4 x 14 1/2 inches
Roger Houston Ogden Collection, New Orleans

Ellsworth Woodward (1861-1939)
Seville, Spain, 1909
watercolor on paper
15 x 11 inches
Roger Houston Ogden Collection, New Orleans

However, much as William excelled with the Raffaelli oil crayon medium, Ellsworth proved to be one of the most brilliant watercolor artists of his time. Large numbers of his watercolors survive from his trips to Europe as well as his sketching expeditions around New Orleans. He had a well-defined, and highly literary, sense of local place which he once expressed in a lecture on the "magic of New Orleans."[12] Speaking of the city, he felt that when an average tourist "found himself wandering in places whose unchanged aspect is a legacy of past centuries; when he sees for the first time the unbelievably fantastic oak swathed in its mournful burden, and palm trees...and when he beholds the full moonrise behind that feathery screen, then indeed is his cup full."

The Woodwards' ultimate contribution to Louisiana's art history really has much more to do with their achievements as organizers of important art movements and institutions than it does with their actual work. Of these, the founding and successful operation of the Newcomb Pottery operation, the establishment of the Art Association of New Orleans from which grew the New Orleans Museum of Art, and the vital research projects on local artists represent the total fulfilling of certain arts and crafts movement ideologies concerning "art and manufacture."

As already noted, the free drawing classes offered by the Woodwards from 1885 to 1894 drew a large and enthusiastic crowd of students, especially women. Never evangelists for "art for art's

Ellsworth Woodward (1861-1939)
Ponte Vecchio, 1912
watercolor on paper
13 x 9 inches
Roger Houston Ogden Collection, New Orleans

Ellsworth Woodward (1861-1939)
Acropolis, 1912
watercolor on paper
8 3/4 x 12 inches
Roger Houston Ogden Collection, New Orleans

sake," the Woodward brothers founded an "arts club...as an outlet for the growing ambitions of the pupils to use their knowledge in some gainful way." William helped to organize Newcomb College in 1886, bringing his brother Ellsworth to teach painting and drawing. Together they helped to found the New Orleans Art Pottery Company, that evolved into the ceramic program at Newcomb by 1894. The pots were thrown by professionals, particularly Joseph Fortune Meyer from 1896 to 1927, with the students decorating and painting them.

Many of the earliest wares of this concern were decorated with highly stylized foliate motifs reminiscent of the languid line of European art nouveau. However, under the lead of Sadie Irvine and Anna Frances Simpson, the decoration evolved towards a more impressionistic palette similar to the shadings of the Woodward brothers' late works. Ellsworth Woodward's evocation of the moon appearing behind a "feathery screen" is well remembered when glimpsing the moss and moon motifs of many of the most prized examples of Newcomb pottery work.

In their history of Newcomb pottery, Suzanne Ormond and Mary Irvine state:

> The real pottery in the public's mind was that with the moss-draped live oak, southern pine, Louisiana cypress, magnolia grandiflora, Louisiana iris, marsh maple, Cherokee rose, day lilies, and water hyacinth always done in odd-number motifs. Ellsworth Woodward, a true nature-lover, would take large groups of students in the spring and fall on field trips to sketch from nature the future designs for the crafts.[13]

It was Woodward, these authors felt, who imparted a genuine love of nature to the students that they never forgot.

Throughout the 1930s Ellsworth Woodward remained a staunch advocate of art education, and a great champion of the rising Southern art movements. Fortunately, many of his lectures and notes were typed up and filed in the Works Progress Administration Collection at the New Orleans Museum of Art. Many of these lectures have a quaint tone which recalls the earnest idealism of the high Victorian era. Woodward remained committed throughout his life to the ideas of solid training in design, and solid application of theoretical techniques to constant, industrious studio activity:

> The failure of art education in most of our colleges may be traced to its theoretical character. Theory does not train the eye and hand nor quicken the personal judgement. In the common schools the wise and effective course unites practice with precept with the aim of awakening the reflective and executive powers, that the individual may be free in the exercise of personal judgement.[14]

Ellsworth Woodward (1861-1939)
Wild Iris, 1908
watercolor
13 x 19 inches
New Orleans Museum of Art, Bequest of Miss Lena Little, 21.8

Woodward made these remarks as early as 1902 in an article on art education for the *Atlantic Educational Journal.*

Woodward had particular regard for the efforts of Southern painters in the twentieth century. Throughout his career as an arts administrator he had been a champion for museums and art colleges in the South. These, he felt sure, would result in a new understanding of Southern culture, and a new respect for the Southern artist. Speaking of these matters Woodward is for once rather startlingly avant-garde. In an article prepared in 1936, at the most fragile moment of Paul Ninas's and John McCrady's efforts at the Arts and Crafts Club, Woodward proved a soulful fellow traveller.

He encouraged his audience to go to contemporary exhibitions:

> If one turns to these exhibitions with his mind possessed by the now outgrown belief that foreign study and the imitation of foreign models are the secrets to excellence in art he will miss what is most important in the work he is studying. But if the observer keeps steadily in view the fact that art is not a commodity, but a vehicle of expression intended to convey what goes on in the mind of the artist reacting to life, he cannot fail to be impressed with recent Southern work. There is in this work a lessening volume of traditional, sentimental, and tritely objective painting, and a growing volume of adventurous struggle toward the expression of ideas and the interpretation of nature and life.[15]

Woodward's remarks herald the arrival of the twentieth century in the arts of Louisiana. By that time he was painting with much less frequency and his brother was reduced to etching his works on a plastic screen for reproduction. Like his brother, Ellsworth Woodward died in 1939.

The art of the Woodward brothers represents one of the most profound chapters in all of Louisiana art. While not native-born, they proved to be far more durable than the legions of itinerants who preceded them. They left behind a legacy of style in art, substance in education, and permanence in institutions.

CHAPTER EIGHT

Representation and Reaction: Louisiana Modernism

As Louisiana entered the twentieth century, the activities of a variety of artists—from the sober, practical Woodward brothers to the colorful and flamboyant old academics like Molinary and Poincy—culminated in the founding and opening of an art museum. The Art Association of New Orleans continued to be a strong group, organizing exhibitions, staging judged shows, and attracting new members from the rising group of young painters in the region. In 1910, with funds given by local sugar magnate Isaac Delgado, an agreement was reached with the City Park Board to build a museum at the terminus point of Esplanade Avenue, which extended from the river to Bayou St. John. From the moment the museum opened, the art world of New Orleans was changed forever.

Before the arrival of the museum, painters and the public had to look to the tides of itinerants for currents of style. After the museum opened, exposure to important national and international art movements became much less dependent upon the attention provoked by the popularity or personality of a particular artist.

It is true that in the first twenty-five years of the museum's life, Ellsworth Woodward exerted a considerable and not always appreciated influence upon public policy. In his recently published history of the New Orleans Museum of Art, Prescott Dunbar is especially critical of Woodward's reluctance to involve the institution in an active acquisition program at a time when "the availability and inexpensiveness of important art works [was] incontestable...."[1] Dunbar's critiques of Woodward are leveled because of his belief that one "of the functions that a public museum is obligated to perform is the acquisition of those artistic treasures by which the citizenry can be enlightened concerning the many art forms or movements of both the past and the present." While this is certainly true, acquisition is not the only means by which the citizenry can be enlightened. The list of exhibitions which the Delgado mounted during the critical years of early modernism in painting movements is impressive for the variety of artists shown, even though some of them have not entered into subsequent histories of note.[2]

Still, local artists did have the opportunity to see works by such noted contemporary artists as John Marin, Pablo Picasso, and Arthur B. Davies. More importantly, these exhibitions indicate that the museum did create an atmosphere in which the important dialectic between representationalism and the emerging schools of objectivism and abstraction could be fully viewed, if not acquired.

Museums have a way of galvanizing free ideas about art into sanctified committees, exhibitions, and acquisitions. To be in a museum collection or to receive a museum show is a sign of approval that most artists working in an urban environment desire to better promote their work.

The rise of a museum dialectic in the cultural life of New Orleans fulfilled the goals of both the old art association academics and the purposeful Woodwards. That it should arrive at a time of great change in styles between the polite didactic compositions of the late nineteenth century and more experimental leanings is a convenient phenomenon for articulating divisions in the community of painters. It is only fair to assume that artists are more likely to respond to the varieties of visual vocabularies than is the public. Art movements emerging on an international scale were certain to find expression in Louisiana.

Consistently, throughout this final period under study, there is an interpolation of styles in Louisiana painting, ranging from the most experimental to the most conservative. Impressionism flourished in the hands of certain old school artists who had been rebels in their youth but found themselves considered passé in their maturity. Young turks created works which offended the public but now seem to be acceptable examples of a well-intentioned modernism. Most importantly in any consideration of local, indigenous movements, several artists began to paint in a style that more truly reflected the conflicts in the local culture. This last group of artists created works of biting social satire cast in terms that were often surreal, and which represent the only substantial assault on the smugness with which the culture of Louisiana in general and New Orleans in particular tends to view itself.

It is well to remember, as we consider Louisiana art in the period 1910-50, that what we see and how the public and critics responded to it are really unlike anything which had previously occurred in the state. Throughout the nineteenth century the primary critical standards for art remained fixated upon some vague, idealistic, and frequently didactic notions about the degree to which any art object responded "truthfully" to nature, or responded with a format that might be proven "useful." So much of the art we have seen so far was created for a very clear demand. Portraiture, landscape art, and genre painting were all obliged to pay some homage to the realities of the world in which they were created, providing accurate perceptions or at least accurate representations. Representationalism, art which looks like some known quantity in the world, and which had been taken for granted up to the twentieth century, was about to become but one part of an expanding and unsettling art equation.

Set against the art of mimesis was art that sought to convey an attitude, or personal expression or impression. As an art form, impressionism, in both its French and American incarnations, was hardly an alien concept to Louisiana. As we have seen, the Woodwards practiced a kind of impressionism. Currency of the style was furthered by exhibitions at the newly opened Delgado Museum, and the activities of various itinerants, who were now referred to as "visiting" artists, wintering in the city.

In 1912 the museum held an impressive showing of French impressionist art from the collections of the distinguished dealers Durand-Ruel of Paris. On display were works by Manet, Monet, and Renoir. Already these paintings, which had seemed truly controversial in the late nineteenth century, had taken on the glow of acceptability dictated by their market value. Clearly, the impressionist approach to color and composition was deemed a proper standard of "modern" art.

To find practicing impressionist artists in New Orleans during these years, one had to go no farther than the lobby of the St. Charles Hotel. During the First World War, the artists Robert Grafton and Louis Oscar Griffith wintered in New Orleans and set up in the lobby, painting murals for the hotel walls and offering both instruction and inspiration for young artists. The works by both have the freshness and clarity of all impressionist art derived from the interaction of primary colors and shadow. Griffith's work in particular has the dazzling quality of Louisiana sunlight, reflected from a thousand sources of water, and shining on the ancient architecture of the French Quarter in an unsettling aura of heat and dust.

In 1917 a young man from Hahnville, Louisiana came to New Orleans and spent the better part of the winter studying and painting with Grafton and Griffith. Clarence Millet had first appeared in New Orleans in 1914, when he worked as an apprentice in an engraving

Robert W. Grafton (1876-1936)
The End Stall, 1916
oil on canvas
24 x 20 inches
New Orleans Museum of Art, Gift of the Art Association of New Orleans, 16.163

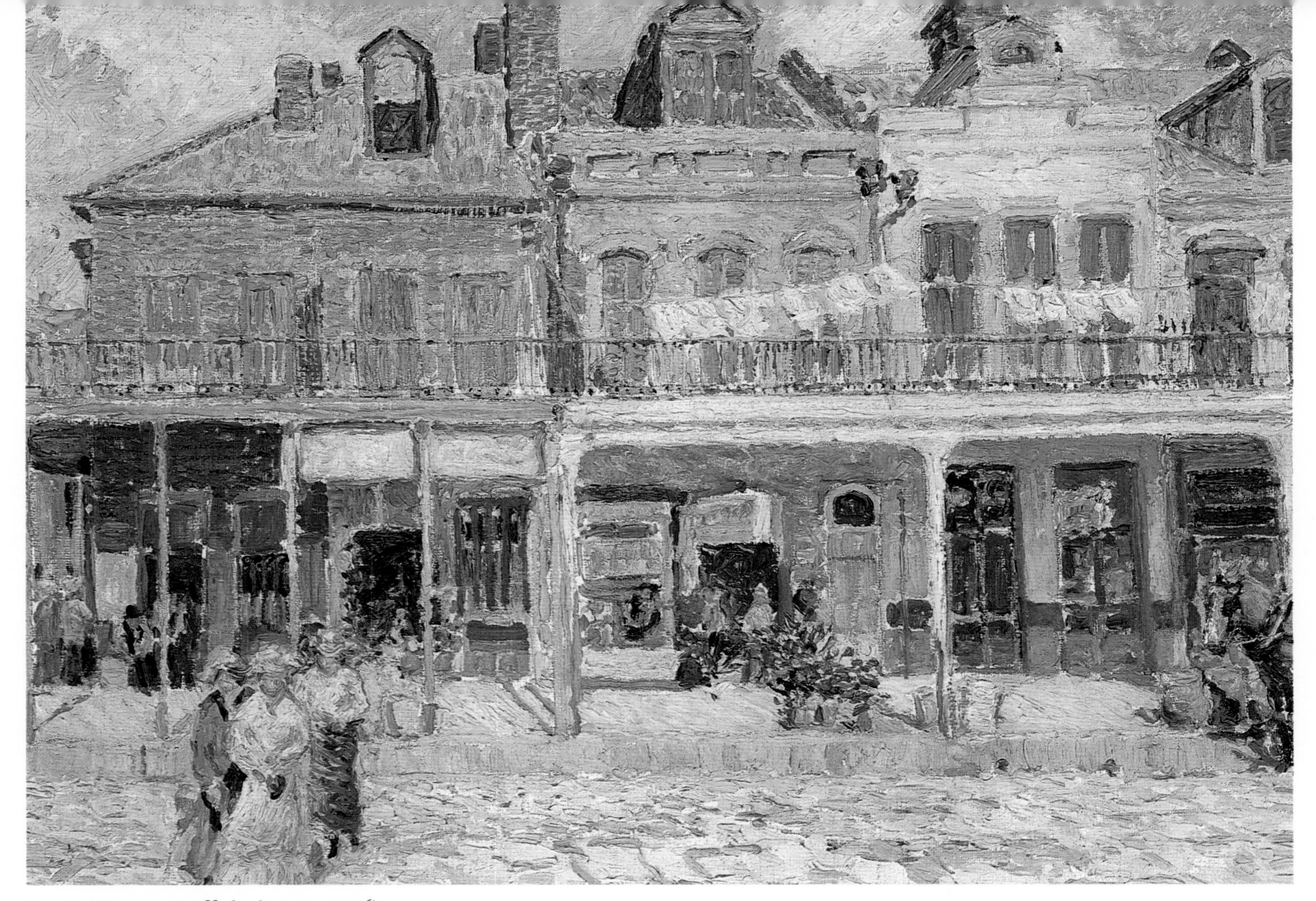

Louis Oscar Griffith (1875-1956)
Begue's Corner, 1916
oil on canvas
18 x 22 inches
New Orleans Museum of Art, Gift of the Art Association of New Orleans, 60.45

company. This was a training he would subsequently utilize by engraving several of his paintings, creating popular prints of the French Quarter to be sold to the persistent tourist trade.

From 1922 until 1924 Millet studied at the Art Students' League in New York. Apparently this instruction consisted primarily of drawing lessons with the academic master George Bridgeman, as subsequent accounts of his painting career indicated that he was "largely self-taught." Bridgeman's instruction in the classical format of drawing may account for the rather bold, simplistic sense of line and the understated compositions of many of the artist's earliest works. Millet often stated that he tried to paint what he saw without elaboration.

In 1924 Millet returned to New Orleans and took up residence at 1225 Galvez Street, his address for the rest of his life. One notice in a 1925 newspaper account states that he was occupying a studio in the same building on Exchange Alley where A. J. Drysdale painted. During these first years as a painter in New Orleans, Millet most often painted the architecture and street life of the Vieux Carré. A notable work of this type is *Antique Shop,* featuring a building on the corner of Chartres and St. Anne streets.

Clarence Millet (1897-1959)
Melon Boats, New Orleans, 1928
oil on canvas
25 x 30 inches
Roger Houston Ogden Collection, New Orleans

Clarence Millet (1897-1959)
New Federal Building
oil on canvas
35 x 29 inches
Baton Rouge Art League Collection, on loan to the Louisiana State Archives

Clarence Millet (1897-1959)
Violet Locks, circa 1950
oil on canvas
27 x 39 inches
Roger Houston Ogden Collection, New Orleans

Millet was a founding member of the Arts and Crafts Club, and taught night classes at their school. Throughout this period he exhibited his work in the South and Northeast, eventually becoming one of the few twentieth-century Southern artists to be elected to the National Academy of Design. During the years of the Great Depression he worked in the easel project of the WPA, and while in that capacity changed his style.

Many American painters during the 1930s abandoned avant-garde art forms for a return to more representational styles and more traditional subject matter, often drawing upon American mythic scenes. At this time Millet began to paint those scenes of plantation houses by moonlight that represent one of the most important bodies of his work. An article written about him and published in the *New Orleanian Magazine* in July 1934 notes that the artist "always seems to concern himself with light, the sparkle of the sun on dancing blue waters, the vivid contrast and tonal values of bright landscapes and sweeping vistas" all painted with "a sense of motion and vigour."

Defying natural order, Millet uses moonlight to the same effect, creating a play of light and shadow as powerful by night as it most certainly would have been by day. This romantic light often fell upon buildings he had observed on site and then transformed into composite constructions. Elizabeth Kell, a critic for the New Orleans *States,* in an article published December 15, 1942 remarked that one of Millet's moonlit houses seemed very familiar "for it is a composite of every abandoned old plantation house I've ever seen."

After the Second World War Millet's recherche oils in the impressionist manner undergo a subtle transformation. His late works are very distinctive in terms of coloration and format. While none of his earlier representational clarity is abandoned, the large curvilinear format of his structures becomes more diffuse. An abstract quality begins to appear, evident in the layers of grey-green coloration defining the marshy riverbank settings of many of these works. From his fledgling work as an impressionist to his late works in a semi-abstract style, Millet remained one of the most important painters working in twentieth-century New Orleans.

Clarence Millet (1897-1959)
Marsh Scene, circa 1950
oil on canvas
26 x 28 inches
Roger Houston Ogden Collection, New Orleans

Young artists working in an impressionist vein were given even greater encouragement and resources for study when Helen Turner reappeared in the city in 1926, after an absence of thirty years. Turner had spent her youth in New Orleans. She was one of the genteel young ladies who had received her initial training in the old art association classes of Molinary and Wikstrom. But in 1896 she went to New York and committed herself to pursuing a life as an artist. She began her formal studies at the Women's branch of the Cooper Union under the tutorship of Kenyon Cox and Douglas Volk.

Neither Cox nor Volk could be considered avant garde under any circumstances, as both worked in what has come to be called the American Renaissance style of the Chicago White City...a reference to the important trends sparked by the Chicago World's Fair of 1893.[3] But the climate of taste in New York during the period was dominated by the successes of American impressionist artists, especially William Merrit Chase. Like several of her contemporaries from the world of Southern women artists, including Kate Freeman Clark and Catherine Wiley, Turner accompanied Chase on a number of his European study trips between 1904 and 1911. On at least one of these trips she witnessed the studio and work of John Singer Sargent.

Art historian Lewis Rabbage has observed that "Helen Turner realized, at least in her later years, that her work was, in a real sense, categorically passé even as it was created."[4] In the sense that Turner worked in what might be called a genteel impressionist vein, this is true. Her work is defined by the typical impressionist fascination with light, and with sensitive and slightly withdrawn female subjects who have the untouchable look of a Cox mural figure. Her virtuoso achievement is color and brushwork, for her slow and diligent manner ensured a finished product of subtlety and warmth.

Turner's reappearance in New Orleans in 1926, at a time when she had all but retired from painting, was not linked to the introduction of more modern trends. She was listed on the Arts and Crafts Club roster of teachers for one year, although it is ironic to think of her there in the presence of such firebrands as John McCrady and Paul Ninas. She painted one portrait, of Matilda Grey, that captures much of the spirit of that fascinating collector and personality. Another composition, *Two Women,* may have been begun in New Orleans, but certainly owes more to the time Turner spent at Cragsmoor, the New York art colony where she spent every summer between 1906 and 1941.

The introduction of nonrepresentational modernism was a slow process which occurred in New Orleans throughout the 1920s and into the first years of the Great Depression. The founding of the Arts and Crafts Club in 1921, and their institution of classes in the French Quarter, ensured an avant-garde spirit which worked as a

Helen Turner (1858-1958)
Two Women, 1926
oil on canvas
40 x 30 1/8 inches
The Museum of Fine Arts, Houston, Museum Purchase with funds provided by the Houston Friends of Art

proper counterbalance to some of the more conservative tendencies of the Delgado Museum. From the outset the club's goals were well defined.[5] The initial roster of officers was composed entirely of women and reads like a social Who's Who. However, its purpose combined the usual genteel idealism "to foster higher artistic standards" with a subtle modern agenda, aiming to "keep members in touch with current literature on arts and crafts...."

The organization was divided into three categories of membership: professionals ("persons actually engaged in works of artistic nature, who must produce one work of art in twelve months at least"), active ("such persons as are interested in the advancement of art"), and sustaining ("such persons as desire to assist individual artists or students in becoming members of the organization").

Initially, the club responded to the international modern movement with the same reluctance which characterized the national attitude. Reactions to the Armory show of 1913 in New York had been very severe, and local organizations for "decency in art" sprang up all over the country. As at no other time in American art, large segments of the artistic community warred with the American public over the purposes and meanings of art. Amidst the great changes represented by the rise of technological culture and the spread of world war, there were those who felt, in the words of Robert Hughes, "that art, in the most disinterested and noble way, could find the necessary metaphors by which a radically changing culture could be explained to its inhabitants."[6]

Such attitudes were deeply resisted in the critical establishment of the New Orleans press. One laudatory review from the *Times-Picayune* of June 7, 1925 actually praises the recent exhibition season of the Arts and Crafts Club for the lack of "so-called 'modernistic' junk." The reviewer further remarked that "here and there someone breaks through with a mis-shapen conglomeration of paint smeared over an otherwise good canvas." What is objectionable about the "so-called 'modernistic'" art is any pretense to insights about "an emotion or somebody's soul." To the fragile group of modernists developing in New Orleans, the critic warned "the art of painting a method of expression of emotions...requires intelligent thought, study and work, and that unless [this] effort possesses the simplicity and unity necessary to convey the same emotion to another, their art is at fault."

These were not isolated thoughts on the part of this one anonymous reviewer. They were also shared by important public figures like Lyle Saxon and Ethel Hutson, who dominated the press reviews of the period. It is small wonder that with this climate of taste, the currents of modernism rarely took a cubist or abstract form in New Orleans or Louisiana. Instead, it developed a caricaturish satiric style, which, as employed by Caroline Durieux or John McCrady, did indeed provide a means for explaining a radically changing culture to its inhabitants...or at least defined in graphic terms the absurdity of that culture.

A primary example of an artist employing the conventions of the Louisiana landscape tradition for a didactic, rather than avant-garde, end is Knute Heldner. Heldner was a twentieth-century itinerant painter. Born in Sweden, he immigrated to Minnesota around the turn of the century, and moved back and forth between Minnesota and New Orleans constantly between 1923 and his death in 1952.

Largely self-taught, Heldner captured the imagination of the New Orleans art establishment with a series of works depicting the eerie swamps and bayous of the surrounding countryside with a

Knute Heldner (born Sweden, 1886-1952)
French Quarter Rooftops from His Studio, 1923
oil on canvas
24 x 22 inches
Roger Houston Ogden Collection, New Orleans

rather unusual vivid blue-green coloration. So successful were these works that Heldner was accepted, acclaimed, and even invited to teach classes at the Arts and Crafts Club after 1927.

In some respects Heldner might be compared to Alexander J. Drysdale, in that both artists were rather formulaic in their approach to landscape. However, where Drysdale concentrated on atmospherics, Heldner was architectonic, situating the same ramshackle cabin in the woods in his works over and over again, varying only in size, quantity of cabins and associative boats, and density of hanging moss.

Heldner did paint a few rather glowingly impressionistic scenes of the Vieux Carré during his first years in New Orleans, as well as some figurative works in a 1930s regionalist style, but these are far rarer than his landscapes.

The Arts and Crafts Club proved to have a historic impact on the teaching of art, and the dissemination of new ideas about what art was all about. The classes provided the best instruction that had ever been offered outside the Woodward classrooms, and the exhibitions proved less conservative with the passing of time. Most importantly, several artists of note in the community found the peer support and financial help they needed to develop along the lines of international modernism. Of these, the most substantial were not born in Louisiana, but arrived there in the exciting decade of the 1920s. The art of Paul Ninas and Will Henry Stevens, although very different in composition, reflects a willingness to experiment and evolve.

Stevens was more academically grounded. A native of Vevay, Indiana, his first art instructions had taken place in the academic environment of the Cincinnati Art Academy, which was still dominated by the teaching of Frank Duveneck and the arts and crafts spirit of the Rookwood pottery movement.[7] In that regard, Stevens' first artworks strongly parallel the example being set in New Orleans by the Woodwards. Perhaps recognizing this, Ellsworth Woodward hired young Stevens to come to New Orleans in 1921 and teach at Newcomb College. Stevens had already been in New Orleans, in order to use "motifs from the old French Quarter for several commissions upon which I am at work...stage settings...."

Stevens' choice of the term "motifs" for architectural details is an accurate description of his approach to painting composition during his early years in New Orleans. His first works in the city have a flat quality and, although representational, do not attempt to project a sense of depth and perspective, but rather divide the plane into interacting fields of color and form, reminiscent of the paintings of Cezanne. Cezanne is really the overarching figure of the modern spirit which moves across many of Stevens' canvases during this period. They are not strongly colored, depending more upon tonal contrasts for figurative variation.

Stevens was hardly a reclusive provincial and his work demonstrates a sure awareness of major national developments. His breaking down of form into strong intersecting lines is reminiscent of the works of the precisionist artists, especially Charles Sheeler. His landscape paintings from the same time have the linear quality one associates with John Marin. Like Marin, Stevens seems to have used this as a springboard out of representational painting and into the realm of color/form abstraction, the medium in which he was quietly, almost secretly, working during the late thirties and forties.

While Stevens travelled widely, he would also have had an ample opportunity for exposure to important trends in nonobjective painting through the auspices of the Arts and Crafts Club. In 1933 that organization sponsored a showing of color reproductions which surveyed the previous fifty years of French painting. Included in that group were the works of Kandinsky and Klee. Their division of the plane into compartmentalized forms, allowing the interaction of amorphous shapes, almost certainly influenced Stevens.

The mature style which emerges from Stevens' brush during his most original period is very similar to that of Kandinsky, Klee, and Arshile Gorky. Those paintings are often described as lyrical. Local critic W. M. Darling found many of these later works, when exhibited at the Arts and Crafts Club gallery in 1945, to be "paintings

Will Henry Stevens (1891-1949)
Abstraction, circa 1940
oil and tempera on masonite
40 1/2 x 34 1/2
New Orleans Museum of Art, Harrod Fund, 46.1

Will Henry Stevens (1891-1949)
Ships in the River, circa 1942
oil on canvas
22 x 30 inches
Roger Houston Ogden Collection, New Orleans

in which not one false note, one error in relationship, asserts itself...absolute harmony prevails." By that point, critical acceptance of modernism was all but assured.

Harmonic is indeed the perfect description for Stevens' work. Though he was obviously concerned with the psychological implications of nonobjective painting, his own work depends upon an interrelationship of color values rather than jarring juxtapositions. His interacting forms, though abstract, are devoid of the undercurrent of disturbance that characterizes so much of the art of the period. This harmony was even appreciated by the *Times-Picayune,* which found that "quietly, with deep feeling and honest presentation, he has imparted an almost universal quality or appeal to his canvases so that they may be understood by any sort of people in any times...." Stevens was a nonconfrontational type of personality, and the search which is evident in his art led many subsequent critics to identify certain abstract, spiritual values in nonrepresentational art.

The art of Paul Ninas, in keeping with the spirit of his life, was confrontational and, for its time, provocative. A native of Missouri, Ninas spent his youth knocking around the country before landing in Paris during the high-water mark of the American expatriate movement. Once there he seems to have met everyone from Alice B. Toklas and Gertrude Stein to Isadora Duncan, who sponsored his first one-man show. From this point Ninas had a professed love for the works of the cubists, tinged with a marked fauvist color obsession.

In the late twenties he bought a coconut plantation in the West Indies, and set about creating an image and career for himself rather like that of Gauguin, painting the native women and giving wildly exotic interviews to visiting correspondents. In one of these he strikes a familiar note in the modernist dialogue:

> The choicer spirits want color and form, to stir their esthetic emotions. Of what significance is a 'speaking' likeness if it has no emotional satisfaction? [8]

Returning to this country for his father's funeral in 1932, Ninas seems to have spontaneously decided to remain in New Orleans, taking up a residence where he was to remain for the rest of his life. Almost immediately he became involved with the Arts and Crafts Club, eventually becoming the principal instructor at the school. Ninas remained with the school for ten years, a period which saw certain gains made in the acceptance and appreciation of modernism, coupled with the return to representational narrative which characterizes so much of so-called regionalist art. By the mid-thirties a critic like Margaret Dixon with the *Morning Advocate* could even allow that a "current show of the New Orleans Arts and Crafts Club includes excellent paintings in the modern manner in addition to several abstractions." She felt that most of the audience viewing the works would be pleased, but admitted that many would "look askance at the abstractions, which will represent nothing at all to most of the visitors."

Most of Ninas's early Louisiana work has an identifiably representational quality. Yet during those first ten years in New Orleans, he slowly evolved towards the analytic cubist approach. Paintings like *Salt Mines, Avery Island* are distinctly in the Cezanne mode, with subtle coloration used to achieve a sense of mass and modelling, and with the same obvious, clean, geometric line giving the entire work an overall unity.

In many respects, Ninas was the most successful painter working in New Orleans in his time. One of his works was sent to the Louisiana pavilion of the World's Fair in New York in 1939, a cartoonish depiction of "Women from a Distant Parish." The critic W. M. Darling praised the "golden brown color, the sculpturesque modeling" of the work. Darling also notes a certain "streamlining" in Ninas's paintings, evidence of art deco leanings. This approach

Paul Ninas (1903-64)
Salt Mines, Avery Island, 1934
oil on canvas
23 x 30 1/2 inches
Roger Houston Ogden Collection, New Orleans

won for Ninas an important commission to paint the murals in the newly renovated Roosevelt Hotel, which remain as one of the most important art deco public murals in Louisiana, and in the country.

Although Ninas's Roosevelt Hotel murals were levee scenes in the old tradition of Sebron and Walker, they were composed with large, rounded, bold figures, and were very highly colored. However, even as he was painting these works it is possible to detect a transition in the artist's style towards greater abstraction. In December 1940, the Delgado Museum opened a major Picasso retrospective organized by the Museum of Modern Art. From this point, Ninas's work becomes increasingly abstract. Many have the feel of analytic cubist landscapes and still lifes, breaking up the surface space into a series of decorative cubes or triangles filled with highly stylized birds and color variations.

It was the style Ninas pursued until his death twenty-four years later, a style that gave him great satisfaction and which represented a creative plateau. Shortly before his death in 1964 he made the prophetic remark that he had "finished two large abstractions in the past two weeks.... I don't know if I will ever again do a complete painting, although I consider these about the best I have done."[9]

Paul Ninas (1903-64)
Dancing Figures, circa 1950
oil on canvas
36 x 45 inches
Roger Houston Ogden Collection, New Orleans

Ninas and his contemporary Josephine Marien Crawford make for rather interesting comparisons. Crawford was a native New Orleanian, from a wealthy and socially prominent uptown family, who began studying in her mid-forties at the Arts and Crafts Club. This was followed by a brief period in 1927 in the Paris studio of Andre Lhote. In Paris Crawford was exposed to certain late, decorative developments in cubism which greatly influenced her style.

Like Picasso and Dufy, in particular, Crawford divided the picture plane into interesting geometric forms which confined, rather than freed, the figure. This ensured a heightened two-dimensionality, denying spatial depth and perspective, enlivened with a delicate coloration.

Crawford was neither pioneer nor herald. Like several Southern women painters of her generation, she returned to the genteel environment of her birth and painted domestic subjects for her own enjoyment. Perhaps the most remarkable of her works is a series of large simplified figural compositions painted on the wallpaper in one of the rooms of her French Quarter residence. While Crawford was certainly a profound artist in her own right, she was, as Richard Stewart has pointed out in his essay for the exhibition catalog

Josephine Marien Crawford (1878-1952)
Two Parrots in Cage, circa 1926-45
oil on canvas
25 3/8 x 20 5/16 inches
The Historic New Orleans Collection, 1978.23.6

Josephine Marien Crawford (1878-1952)
Milliner's Shop (Woman Sewing Baby Bonnets), 1934-35
oil on canvas
27 1/2 x 35 1/2 inches
The Historic New Orleans Collection

Josephine Marien Crawford (1878-1952)
Self Portrait, circa 1927-28
oil on board
19 1/4 x 13 3/4 inches
The Southeastern Newspaper Corporation Collection on loan to the Morris Museum of Art, Augusta, Georgia

Painting in the South, a recluse whose "modern style was not, in the end, fully accomplished or lastingly influential."

Even as Paul Ninas, Will Henry Stevens, and Josephine Crawford were exploring the spatial possibilities of two-dimensional analytic cubism, pressing economic and social factors were prompting another art dialogue in the larger world which had several impressive manifestations in Louisiana. The advent of the Great Depression, with the stock market crash of 1929, had a beneficial side for many painters. In conjunction with the Works Progress Administration, an easel and mural painting project was established in Louisiana which employed many of the most talented artists of the time, including Clarence Millet, Gideon Townsend Stanton, Caroline Wogan Durieux, Bill Perkins, Edwin Schoenberger, and Perkins Harnly.

Perkins Harnly (born 1901)
New Orleans Cemetery, circa 1937
watercolor on paper
22 1/4 x 17 1/2 inches
Private Collection, San Francisco

The unsettling aspects of the economic travail had prompted many artists, especially the Midwest regionalists and the more avant-garde New York social realists, to reassess the American democratic experiment in more traditional terms. Paintings like those of the celebrated Grant Wood from Iowa, whose *American Gothic* approaches the status of a religious icon, were "fables for hard times" in the words of his biographer Wanda Corn.[10] By "assuring Americans...that they had a collective identity and a shared past," many paintings in the WPA, regionalist style represented a full-fledged retreat from the modernist, abstract onslaught. Deeply conservative critics like Thomas Craven lauded this retrenchment on the national scale: "A battle has been waged and won, a decisive victory over provincial ignorance, anemic imitation, cheap internationalism, and the post war hang-over of esthetic snobbery."[11]

While nothing quite so dramatic was happening in Louisiana, some very interesting paintings were being created. The easel project began in 1935, initially presided over by Ellsworth Woodward and Gideon Townsend Stanton. Stanton was a native of Morris, Minnesota who had moved with his family to New Orleans at the age of three.

He began his career as a stock broker, pursuing art on the side until 1907, when he began to exhibit locally in New Orleans. His first works were very much in the older style of the academic associations, but his deep involvement in the art community ensured a steady growth and maturation of style. He served as a trustee for the Delgado Museum until his appointment to the Louisiana WPA project in 1935.

Like many paintings in the social realist mode, his composition is grounded in very traditional drafting devices, juxtaposing large rounded forms with flat angular spaces. Stanton's most sophisticated work, as in *Two Female Figures,* is very much in keeping with certain tenets established by Kenneth Hayes Miller and other New

Gideon Townsend Stanton (1885-1964)
Two Female Figures
oil on canvas
26 x 24 inches
Ronnie and Joseph Brenner Collection, New Orleans

York artists working in the figurative style of the Cooper Union school.

Richard Cox's observation, in a catalog of Louisiana WPA art, that "what we do not find in...these paintings is perhaps more revealing than what is there," is a crucial critical insight.[12] Cox, and his fellow authors, felt that "Louisiana artists stood outside the national debate over the proper direction of American Realist art," shunning the role of the artist as an instrument of social change. Instead, what one sees in their art is "lots of local color and charm and engaging proletariate types who seem to thrive rather than suffer in their dingy neighborhoods."

Edwin Schoenberger (1915-?)
Ice House Stack
oil on canvas
30 1/8 x 25 inches
Baton Rouge Art League Collection, on loan to the Louisiana State Archives

These remarks are certainly true when one is considering rather straightforward works like Schoenberger's *Ice House Stack* and Perkins' *Checker Game*. In neither of these works is there an obvious political agenda or social critique. Both paintings are excellent examples of their type. Schoenberger evokes the sharply angular precisionist works of Charles Sheeler and Charles Demuth, bringing a highly sophisticated style to Louisiana at a time when only Ralston Crawford's photographs found similar possibilities in the unique visual environment of the state.

The WPA art program in Louisiana was never very large; Cox reports that there were never more than thirty-five painters working on the easel project. However, when considered with other modernist developments in Louisiana it did provide a setting for introducing important national trends into the state, even if those trends did not always reflect the pressing social concerns identified by others. The small number of WPA works preserved by the Baton Rouge Arts League is most impressive as an indication of the range of painterly activity, and heralds the rise of a far more vibrant contemporary art scene following the Second World War.

William Perkins (?-1966)
Checker Game
oil on canvas
22 1/8 x 26 1/4 inches
Baton Rouge Art League Collection, on loan to the Louisiana State Archives

One by-product of the WPA was the revival of the mural painting tradition in public buildings, a revival sparked by federal funding. In this arena Louisiana was ahead of the times, for Huey Long's building programs in Baton Rouge included mural work in several reception areas and courtrooms. Several of these commissions were carried out by the artist Conrad Albrizio. Albrizio was a native New Yorker of Italian descent who settled in New Orleans during the 1920s.[13]

Albrizio received his first mural commission from Long in 1931, producing a series of works with allegorical themes. At the same time he was painting a number of works in the regionalist style. One of these, *Jordan* or *River Baptism,* is considered to be one of Albrizio's finest paintings.

Jordan depicts a group of blacks on the banks of a river witnessing a baptismal scene. The figures writhe exuberantly as they celebrate the event. As a scene in which black subjects are painted with a certain allegorical intention, it represents a serious departure from previous imagery. The figures are painted with great muscular clarity, not as simple allegorical figures but as individuals

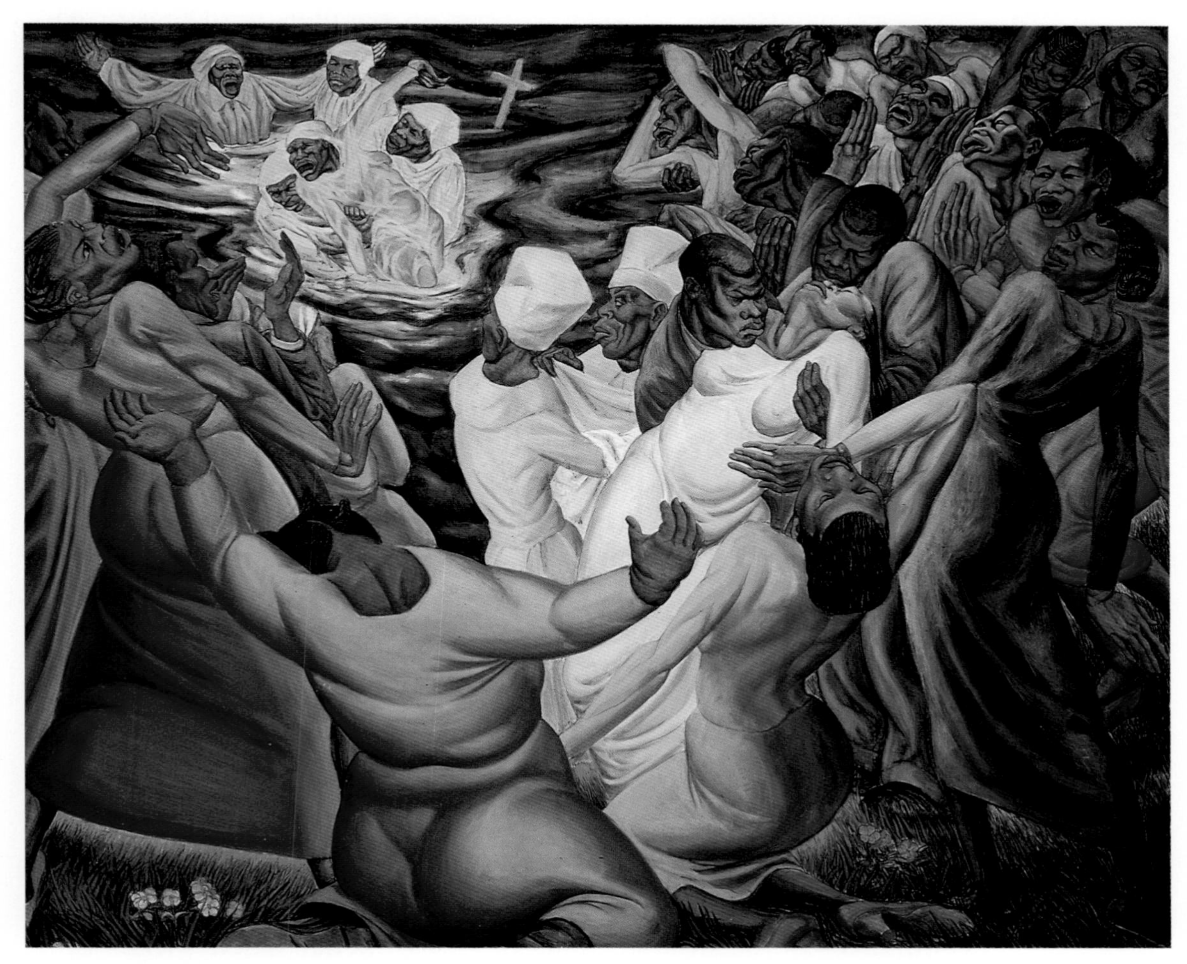

Conrad Albrizio (1894-1973)
Jordan, 1935-37
tempera on board
40 x 48 inches
Louisiana Arts and Science Center, Baton Rouge, Louisiana

Daniel Webster Whitney (1898-1965)
The Place, 1942
oil on canvas
30 x 20 inches
The Historic New Orleans Collection, 1986.196.8

who happen to be black. They are more subject to the strange rhythms of religion and mannered composition, than to social concerns.

In 1935 Albrizio was appointed to the faculty at Louisiana State University, a move which ensured a vital modernist presence there. Eventually Caroline Durieux would join the same faculty and, together with serious developments in the English department, create one of the strongholds of the Southern cultural renaissance. Albrizio moved towards more expressionistic abstractions during the forties, while continuing to pursue his career as a muralist.

By the late 1940s, the abstract mode, whether free form or rendered in analytic cubist style, had come to dominate the art world of Louisiana, completing a national trend. Young artists like Douglas Brown and Daniel Webster Whitney were developing this style just as the period under study was drawing to a close. Whitney's early death prevented his complete maturation as a painter, yet the works extant indicate a concentrated style moving away from the control of analytic cubism and towards amorphous postpainterly abstraction. His work is an omen of the artistic atmosphere of the 1950s, just beyond the reach of this study.

Douglas Brown's career has certain parallels with that of Paul Ninas. He was a penniless drifter in New Orleans in 1927 when the sight of a broken levee inspired him to embark upon the creation of visual images very much in the precisionist mode. His works tend to fracture architectonic forms into hard-edged geometric solidities painted in primary colors. After he began to paint, Brown achieved far greater success in the Northeast, although he did return to New Orleans several times in the period under study. He often exhibited at the Arts and Crafts Club and with the artists of the Federal Arts Project.

Remarks by previous art historians about the lack of substance in early twentieth-century art in Louisiana are not altogether correct. Many have sought, in this state's art, evidence of an obvious response to modernism, a movement which was, after all, European in origin and dominated by obscure French and German traditions. There is an original art movement in Louisiana during the very period under consideration which deserves far greater attention, and a lens wiped clean of the same provincial antiquarianism which continues to haunt all Southern studies.

At the same time that abstraction was finding shallow soil in Louisiana, surrealism was more than adequately nourished. Combining sense of place with an absurdist regard for manners and mores, artists like Elizabeth Laughlin, Caroline Durieux, John McCrady, and Walter Anderson created unique works outside the canons of established international movements. Their pieces offer a vision of the local terrain as profound as the light-intense effort of the first generation of landscape artists.

Douglas Brown (dates unknown)
The Red Building
watercolor on paper
14 x 21 5/8 inches
Private Collection, San Francisco

Elizabeth Laughlin (born 1914)
Flight of the Flowers, 1949
oil on canvas
47 1/2 x 53 inches
Elizabeth Heintzen Laughlin Collection, New Orleans

Elizabeth Laughlin was the wife of the surrealist photographer Clarence John Laughlin. His work transformed the ruins of the Louisiana antebellum plantation world into a metaphor for the visitations of time upon the evolving human spirit. Elizabeth Laughlin's still life works have a great clarity of form, vivid coloration, and unsettling, spiraling compositions quite unlike anything else being painted in her time. This strain of individualism is apparent in the works of several of her contemporaries, at a time when personal style seems to have been more important to the artistic community of Louisiana than responding to national or international art trends.

Although Walter Anderson is most often associated with the Mississippi Gulf Coast, he was born in New Orleans and grew up in a house on the corner of St. Charles and Broadway. His mother, Annette McConnell Anderson, was also an artist and had studied with the Woodward brothers at the Newcomb School of Art. Her vaguely impressionistic works have a soft warm coloring and strong sense of design, the very elements many critics have admired in the works of her son. Young Anderson was well acquainted with the Woodwards, visiting William at his Gulf Coast home several times after his removal there during the 1920s.

Walter Anderson studied in New York, at the Parsons School of Design, and in the studio program of the Pennsylvania Academy of Fine Arts. Upon his inherent Deep South impressionist mentality and palette he built a considerable academic expertise. Anderson's compositional approach was brilliant, indeed one of the most original and innovative in the history of any artist working in Louisiana. Unfortunately, after his return to the Gulf Coast area during the Depression, and his marriage, he began to exhibit schizophrenic tendencies and was hospitalized on several occasions.

For the most part Anderson dealt with the natural world of the Ocean Springs, Mississippi, area.[14] However, he made several trips to New Orleans, producing a substantial number of large-scale watercolors from his experiences. These watercolors fulfill previously discussed longings on the part of several art historians for evidence of social concerns, and more importantly, social realism, in indigenous Louisiana art. More importantly, perhaps, they were produced by an artist whose strangely skewed view of the world gave those works a slightly surreal edge. The most significant body of work was the result of a New Orleans trip Anderson made in 1943, a trip he recorded in a journal which has survived.[15]

Like all of his writing, it has a certain directness, a childlike love of adventure, and a very serious appreciation of the world's natural splendors. A curious consistency emerges in this journal, very much in keeping with the modernist sense of proportion. No single event plays a dominant role, and equal weight is given to episodes of substance and seemingly inconsequential activities.

Anderson undertook the 1943 trip on a bicycle, riding from Ocean Springs to New Orleans by way of the Rigolets, a route which preceded the construction of the Lake Pontchartrain bridge. Arriving in New Orleans, he set up on Canal Street. The forms and movement of the people on Canal Street attracted him, and he sat down to draw what he saw: "I had the good fortune to find a packing case...sat on that and drew people all morning."

These drawings, and the subsequent watercolors, fall into several general categories, reflecting those things in the city which interested Anderson and which he records in the journal.[16] Crowds and cars, the Algiers ferry, architectural renderings, and signs all drew his eye. The ferry held a special attraction because it could transport him to the other side of the river, where he swam and observed a group of little black boys whose "dark bodies against the sky" he found "beautiful." On his second day, instead of returning to Canal Street, he "tried the business section and did buildings and walking business men." He enjoyed working in this area, and found the architectural detail "stimulating for some reason."

The works of art which resulted from this stimulation have a very heightened sense of scale and perspective. The sides of the tall buildings of the business district loom like the walls of a giant canyon, sliding down the harsh diagonal orientation line of the picture plane. As they are painted in bright yellow tones, it is as

Walter Anderson (1903-65)
Crowds on Canal
oil on panel
24 x 24 inches
Estate of the Artist, Ocean Springs, Mississippi

if the reflection of the sun had gilded the elaborately wrought surfaces, transforming them into structures of imposing dignity.

The definition of their architecture is carried over into the images of pedestrians walking about the city. In a finite number of steps, and occupying a hieratic position, the often faceless but distinct individuals walk the streets in a pattern that is anything but the spontaneous movement of normal shoppers and city workers. In the drawings of people on Canal Street, or in the business district, there is a sense of conformity.

In one drawing, the hats in the shop window mirror the position of the hats upon the heads of the passersby. This is an art that is clearly a formal imitation of life, and the life at hand is a mirror image of the conformity of the commercial, urban world. The conclusion that Anderson felt a sense of alienation, and even resentment at the anonymity of the swarming sea of humanity about him, is to be expected, though perhaps it rings a little too loudly of Thoreau and the romantic idyll.

Corroborating that conclusion is the way in which the faces of the pedestrians are drawn. They are mere masks, devoid of deeper human expression, locked in slight frowns. Some of them simply stare vacantly into the distance.

In many respects Anderson's art is as deceptively simple, and therefore elusive, as the art of Vincent van Gogh. Both were more than slightly disconnected from this world, and although this may be a suitable role for the artist, the burden of mental illness lends their work a passionate intensity which transcends the pretty flowers, ripe fields, and gentle wildlife they loved to paint.

Anderson's art is not a mirror of nature, or urban existentialism. It is a reflection of what he saw in the mirror, and what he was able to render with superb craft and a highly appealing visual awareness. A man of divided sensibilities, he was also a man of great personal insight. "Man must possess the extremes within himself...the means too, but certainly the extremes, which form his limits," he once wrote.

In Anderson, we can see how the mental state of the artist bares itself in the demanding personalism of modernism. As we have previously noted, a variety of artists from the nineteenth century, not the least of whom were Harold Rudolph and Richard Clague, suffered from depression, anxiety, and what might currently be called schizophrenia. Yet none of this is reflected in their art. Considering that much of modernism is a bifurcated response to states of being and imagination, it is altogether fitting that Anderson created a personal vision from his perceptions of the Louisiana scene. In that regard he is not unlike Durieux and McCrady, although the latter two always had a more literary agenda bordering on the confessional and the satiric.

Caroline Wogan Durieux was born in New Orleans to a family that combined French Creole and Yankee ancestry. Again, these are divisions which proved quite useful in satirizing the Creole society of New Orleans as well as the pitfalls and general gaudiness of modern life. Her initial training at Newcomb, with Ellsworth Woodward, is said to have been in a tradition she disliked. Miss Wogan's artistic horizon was expanded by her studies at the Pennsylvania Academy of Fine Arts in Philadelphia with Henry McCarter and Arthur B. Carles. This was a time when more up-to-date schools were moving beyond impressionism to the various spirits of symbolism, abstraction, and the streamlined *art moderne*.

After her marriage to import-export businessman Pierre Durieux in 1920, Caroline Durieux lived in Havana, Cuba. There she worked as a designer until her husband was transferred to Mexico City, where she was to remain until 1937. The move to Mexico City was a critical event in her life, for while there she met the radical Mexican muralist Diego Rivera. Rivera's large, bold figures became

Caroline Durieux (1896-1989)
Cafe Tupinamba, 1934
oil on canvas
32 x 40 inches
The Walker Ronaldson Collection, New Orleans

Caroline Durieux (1896-1989)
Acolytes, 1935
oil on canvas
24 x 24 inches
Roger Houston Ogden Collection, New Orleans

a part of Durieux's canon, and his powerful observations of the human condition deeply influenced her subsequent works.

While in Mexico she began to make prints, the medium for which she is best known. In this pursuit she was encouraged by Carl Zigrosser. Combining the social realism of Rivera with her own whimsical sense of satire, she began to produce work that was well accepted when exhibited in New Orleans, New York, and Mexico City. Much of this work was reproduced in a volume called *43 Lithographs and Drawings,* published by LSU Press, which won the National Book Award for 1949.

By 1937 Durieux had returned to New Orleans, replacing Ellsworth Woodward and Gideon Stanton on the WPA. She produced a number of her best-known works for the WPA guide to Louisiana, many of which used Mardi Gras as subject matter. The surrealism of costumes and masks appealed to her sense of the absurd, and conveyed a subtle message about the importance of style over substance in the slightly hysterical world of New Orleans.

From 1937 until 1943 Durieux taught at Newcomb. In 1943 she accepted a position at LSU, where she was to remain for the rest of her career. While there she developed several innovative printmaking techniques.

Caroline Durieux is one of the most admired figures of twentieth-century Louisiana art. Her style and approach seem perfectly suited to the ribald, decadent, and pretentious society of old New Orleans that she loved very deeply. Ray Samuel, in an article on Durieux's works in 1949, wrote:

> There is a symbolism in her work, an undercurrent of feeling, both expressed and implied which the casual observer often misses. This...is the real Durieux, for she takes pleasure in contrasting the superficial and the solid. If humor creeps in, fine, but hers is to laugh and not to laugh.

John McCrady shared Durieux's appreciation of Mardi Gras as an inspired source for subject matter. After the sharp criticisms he received in 1946 for his depictions of black life, McCrady turned increasingly to local scenes in New Orleans. Experimenting with modern forms, McCrady produced a series of works based on Mardi Gras which were used, along with those of Durieux and Ralph Wickiser, in a volume published in 1948 called *Mardi Gras Day*.

One McCrady painting, *The Parade,* was completed in 1950, the final year of this study. It continues a thematic approach which McCrady created in the 1930s, using cutaway buildings and an ironic juxtaposition of external revelry and internal contemplation. The cutaway building in this work is closely related to a painting finished in 1948, *I Can't Sleep,* which also reveals the interior action in a French Quarter dwelling.

Slicing the building has an interesting corollary in certain avant-garde theatrical productions, notably the first performance of Tennessee Williams' *Glass Menagerie*. McCrady peoples the work

John McCrady (1911-68)
The Parade, 1950
multistage on canvas
20 x 39 1/2 inches
Roger Houston Ogden Collection, New Orleans

with figures from his more regionalist work. The dancing figures on the top floor, interconnected and making a wide circle, are not unlike the figures in *Boys Playing* or *Steamboat 'round the Bend.* An autobiographical note is added by the presence of the artist in several of these paintings, attempting to work in the midst of the revelry.

McCrady's most important painting, *The Shooting of Huey Long,* is also one of the few works from the period that profoundly responds, in both technique and narration, to a critical contemporary event. At once violent and cartoonish, the painting depicts Long at the moment of his shooting, gazing at an unseen audience, even as his assassin, Dr. Carl A. Weiss, Jr., is being riddled with bullets in the background. The combination of frenzy, bloodied bodies, and chaos is set in the symbolic art deco architecture of the Louisiana State Capitol that Long built when governor. It is an absurd image worthy of both the event and the individual lost and lamented.

John McCrady (1911-68)
The Shooting of Huey Long, 1939
multistage on canvas
40 x 30 inches
Mr. and Mrs. Keith C. Marshall Collection, New Orleans

McCrady's brilliance rested in his ability to infuse his narrative works with a lush subliminal intent strengthened by virtuous technique and an innovative compositional approach. Two of his contemporaries could have profited from his example. Weeks Hall and Boyd Cruise responded to the implications, both visual and historical, of the Louisiana scene, yet in exactly opposite directions.

Weeks Hall was the descendant of an old Louisiana plantation family from New Iberia, who spent part of his young adult life in avant-garde art circles in the Northeast, studying in Philadelphia and Europe. He returned to New Iberia to restore the family home, Shadows-on-the-Teche, to something of its antebellum splendor. In many respects Hall was a typical example of the Southern grotesque—haunted by the past, prone to decadence, and a committed romantic, despite all appearances. His *Self-Portrait,* drunk and overshadowed by an empty canopied bed, is a conception worthy of Tennessee Williams and Truman Capote, who later explored many of the same themes.

Boyd Cruise, on the other hand, was a serious representational artist with a strong illustrative bent. Cruise was born in Mississippi, but grew up in Lake Charles, Louisiana. His first work, as a window decorator in New Orleans, set the tone of much of his subsequent artistic work: lush, evocative, and entirely fictitious depictions of the antebellum architecture of the Vieux Carré and the Garden District.

In Cruise's carefully detailed watercolor paintings of architecture, there is no decay, no squalor, no person who is not pretty—absolutely no brush with reality. He does capture the architectural substance of the locale with great finesse, recalling the work of the nineteenth-century draftsman Adrien Persac. In addition Cruise painted exquisitely rendered still lifes of great style and precision.

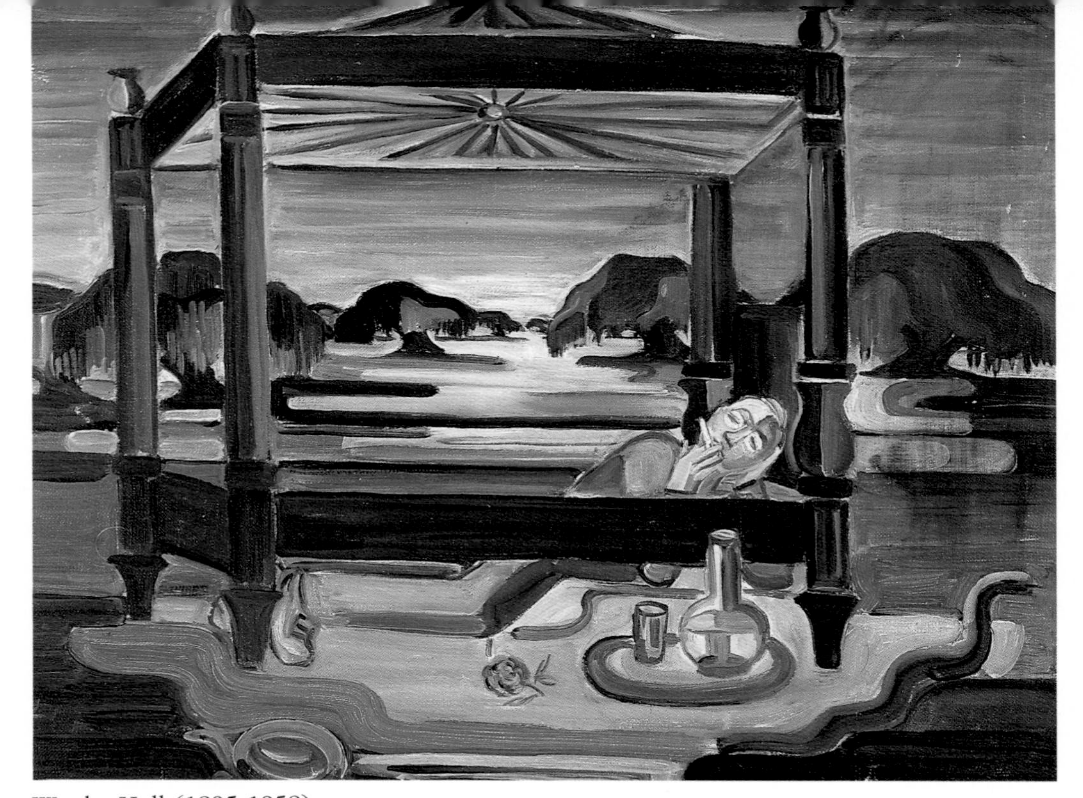

Weeks Hall (1895-1958)
Self-Portrait, circa 1930
oil on canvas
15 x 18 inches
The Historic New Orleans Collection, 1986.192.1

Weeks Hall (1895-1958)
Brown Magnolia, 1940
oil on masonite
13 7/8 x 17 inches
New Orleans Museum of Art, Gift of the Arts and Crafts Club of New Orleans, 41.1

Boyd Cruise (1909-88)
Red Plums, 1949
watercolor on paper
14 3/4 x 13 7/8 inches
Anglo-American Museum, Louisiana State University, Baton Rouge, Gift of Milton Womack in memory of his wife, Barbara Sevier Womack

Marion Souchon (1871-1954)
Permanent Address
oil on board
30 x 32 inches
New Orleans Museum of Art, Lillian and Jeff Feibleman Collection

Ralph Wright Brewer (1901-75)
Anxious Lonely Trees, circa 1950
oil on canvas
26 x 38 inches
The Forster Brewer Collection

Most of his works were either commissioned or sponsored by Gen. and Mrs. Kemper Williams, founders of the Historic New Orleans Collection.

More than any other artist Boyd Cruise reflects the very soul of Louisiana caught between past and present, reality and sentiment. The strong tides of social realism which pervaded the works of writers such as George Washington Cable and later William Faulkner wash over Cruise without effect. So do the symbolic, bathetic efforts of John McCrady and Tennessee Williams. Cruise's art is the art of window dressing, an art which represents a strong current in the narrative river of Louisiana art.

With these late works, by a variety of artists, the use of Louisiana as subject matter comes to a rather lush maturation. Especially in the New Orleans French Quarter, time gradually moved the painter from itinerant portraitist to landscape painter for the tourist trade to freely functioning modernist. The history of art is the history of style, and opportunity. Art appreciation is another matter altogether. It does not divide painting into competing camps, but views each work in the same way one might have viewed a line of steamboats bunched on the levee. They were washed downriver to this place, gathered spontaneously by the powerful draw of their principal reason for being.

NOTES

PREFACE

1. Estill Curtis Pennington, *Look Away: Reality and Sentiment in Southern Art*. (Atlanta: 1989).

2. Barbara Novak, *American Painting of the Nineteenth Century*. (New York: 1969), 10.

3. Erwin Panofsky, *Meaning in the Visual Arts*. (Chicago: 1955), 55.

4. Leon Battista Alberti, *On Painting*, trans. John R. Spencer (New Haven: 1966), 40.

CHAPTER ONE

1. See artist's files and *Encyclopaedia of New Orleans Artists 1718-1918* (New Orleans: 1987) in the Historic New Orleans Collection.

2. Shirley Ann Grau, "Foreword" in *Old Creole Days*, George Washington Cable (New York: 1961), ix.

3. George David Coulon, "Old Painters in New Orleans," MLS, Louisiana State Museum, scrapbook no. 100. All further quotations from Coulon are from this source.

4. Charles Etienne Arthur Gayarré, *Romance of the History of New Orleans* (New York: 1848).

5. Joe Gray Taylor, *Louisiana* (New York: 1976), 16.

6. Henry Rightor, *Standard History of New Orleans, Louisiana* (Chicago: 1900), 20.

7. Ibid.

8. Mathias James O'Connor, *Journals* (May 24, 1789), as recorded by the American Catholic Historical Society of Philadelphia, with copies in the Historic New Orleans Collection.

9. Richard H. Saunders and Ellen G. Miles, *American Colonial Portraits: 1700-1776* (Washington: 1987), 237.

10. Pal Lelman, *Peruvian Colonial Painting* (Brooklyn: 1971).

11. John Burton Harter and Mary Louise Tucker, *The Louisiana Portrait Gallery Volume 1 to 1870* (New Orleans: 1979), 22.

12. Minutes of the Cabildo, iv, no. 3 (July 21, 1797): 3.

CHAPTER TWO

1. Henry Adams, *History of the United States of America During the Administrations of Jefferson & Madison* (New York: 1986), 574.

2. Novak, *American Painting of the Nineteenth Century*, 119-20.

3. For a complete account of West's life and art, see Estill Curtis Pennington, *William Edward West (1788-1857): Kentucky Painter* (Washington, D.C.: 1985).

4. William Dunlap, *A History of the Rise and Progress of the Arts of Design in the United States* (New York: 1969), 320.

5. Donald Culross Peattie, ed., *Audubon's America: The Narratives and Experiences of John James Audubon* (Boston: 1940), 160.

6. New Orleans *Courier*, 1 March 1820.

7. New Orleans *Courier*, 28 July 1820.

8. Howard Corning, ed., *Journal of John James Audubon Made during His Visit to New Orleans in 1820-21* (Boston: 1929).

9. Harold Edward Dickson, *John Wesley Jarvis, American Painter, 1780-1840: With a Checklist of His Works* (New York: 1949).

10. William H. Gerdts, *The Art of Henry Inman* (Washington, D.C.: 1987), 31.

11. Peattie, *Audubon's America,* 136, 162, 163-65, 167.

12. William Barrow Floyd, *Jouett-Bush-Frazer, Early Kentucky Artists* (Lexington: 1968), 169-77. All subsequent quotes from Jouett concerning Stuart are taken from this text.

13. See Robert Bishop, *Folk Painters of America* (New York: 1979).

14. *Louisiana Scrapbook,* vol. 1, New Orleans Public Library, 114.

15. Matthew Harris Jouett to Thomas Sully, ALS, 12 November 1822, Historical Society of Pennsylvania, Philadelphia.

16. Lynne W. Farwell, *Jean Joseph Vaudechamp* (New Orleans: 1967).

17. Sidney Louis Villere, *Jacques Philippe Villere* (New Orleans: 1981), 115.

18. Dunlap, *A History of the Arts in the United States,* 471.

19. Judge James C. Moise, "Theodore S. Moise," MLS, April 1900, Louisiana State Museum, scrapbook no. 100.

20. Judith Hopkins Bonner, "George David Coulon: A Nineteenth Century French Louisiana Painter," in *In Old New Orleans,* ed. W. Kenneth Holditch (Jackson: 1983), 41-61.

21. Lyle Saxon, *Old Louisiana* (New Orleans: The Century Co., 1929). Reprint (New Orleans: Pelican Publishing Company, 1988), 140.

22. See William H. Gerdts, "Natural Aristocrats in a Democracy," in *American Portraits in the Grand Manner* (Los Angeles: 1981), 27-60.

CHAPTER THREE

1. For an interesting account of early landscape art in the lower Mississippi Valley, accompanied by text drawn from contemporary sources, see the exhibition catalog "Mississippi Panorama" (St. Louis: 1950).

2. Kenneth Clark, *Ruskin Today* (London: 1964), 146.

3. Edward J. Nygren, *Views and Visions* (Washington, D.C.: 1986), 3.

4. Anglo-American Museum, "The Louisiana Landscape, 1800-1969" (Baton Rouge: 1969), 16.

5. New Orleans *Argus,* 20 March 1826.

6. See John Wilmerding et al., *American Light, The Luminist Movement 1850-1875* (Princeton: 1989), for a complete account of the development of the luminist theory and interpretation of American landscape art.

7. Novak, *American Painting of the Nineteenth Century,* 96.

8. T. Addison Richards, "The Landscape of the South," *Harper's New Monthly Magazine* 6 (May 1853): 721-33.

9. New Orleans *Daily Picayune,* 30 March 1859.

10. *Catalog of the Collection of Paintings and Other Works of Art belonging to James Robb, Esq.* (New Orleans: 1859), 7.

11. J. A. Dacus and James W. Buel, *A Tour of St. Louis, or The Inside Life of a Great City* (St. Louis: 1878), 73.

12. Joseph Rusling Meeker, "Some Account of the Old and New Masters," in *American Painters,* G. W. Sheldon (New York: 1879), 135-38.

13. Henry Wadsworth Longfellow, *The Poetical Works of Longfellow* (Boston: 1975), 85.

14. Roulhac Toledano, *Richard Clague 1821-1873* (New Orleans: 1974), 29.

15. Peter Bermingham, *American Art in the Barbizon Mood* (Washington, D.C.: 1975), 14.

16. Wilmerding, *American Light,* 109.

17. Richard Clague's sketchbooks were purchased at auction after his death by Marshall J. Smith, Sr., and presented to his son, Marshall J. Smith, Jr., the artist. They are now in the collection of the New Orleans Museum of Art.

18. The work is now in the collection of Mr. W. E. Groves of New Orleans.

19. Howard Buechner, *Drysdale 1870-1934, Artist of Myth and Legend* (Metairie, La.: 1985).

CHAPTER FOUR

1. Samuel Wilson, Jr., ed., *Southern Travels: Journal of John H. B. Latrobe 1834* (New Orleans: 1986), 36.

2. See Perry T. Rathbone, ed., *Mississippi Panorama* (St. Louis: 1950).

3. Mark Twain, *Life on the Mississippi* (New York: 1961), 109.

4. Ray Samuel, in *Currier & Ives Chronicles of America,* ed. John Lowell Pratt (Maplewood, New Jersey: 1968), 190.

5. A. Persac's map, "Plantations on the Mississippi River: From Natchez to New Orleans," is still distributed today by Pelican Publishing Company in Gretna, Louisiana.

CHAPTER FIVE

1. Thomas Marc Fieher, "The African Presence in Colonial Louisiana: An Essay on the Continuity of Caribbean Culture," in *Louisiana's Black Heritage* (New Orleans: 1979), 3-31.

2. Charles Edward O'Neill, S.J., "Fine Arts and Literature: Nineteenth Century Louisiana Black Artists and Authors," in *Louisiana's Black Heritage,* 71-78.

3. Ulrich Bonnel Phillips, "The Central Theme of Southern History," in *The Slave Economy of the Old South* (Baton Rouge: 1968), 275.

4. Eugene Genovese, *Roll Jordan Roll* (New York: 1976), 194.

5. See Estill Curtis Pennington, "Moss Hung and Moonlit: Currier & Ives and the Old South Cult," in *Proceedings of the North American Print Conference* (1990).

6. James J. A. Fortier, ed., *Carpet-Bag Misrule in Louisiana* (New Orleans: 1938), 5.

7. Keith Marshall, *John McCrady, 1911-1968* (New Orleans: 1975), 43.

8. James L. Wilson, *Clementine Hunter: American Folk Artist* (Gretna, La.: Pelican Publishing Company, 1988), 19-32. Saxon's *Old Louisiana* is also published by Pelican.

CHAPTER SIX

1. Edward King, *The Great South* (Hartford: 1875), 40.

2. See Estill Curtis Pennington, *The* Last Meeting's *Lost Cause* (Spartanburg, S.C.: 1988).

3. August P. Trovaioli and Roulhac B. Toledano, *William Aiken Walker, Southern Genre Painter* (Baton Rouge: 1972), 56.

4. See Patrick J. Geary, ed., *Leon Fremaux's New Orleans Characters* (Gretna, LA: Pelican Publishing Company, 1987).

5. See Doreen Bolger, "The Education of the American Artist," in *The Pennsylvania Academy of Fine Arts, 1805-1976* (Philadelphia: 1976).

6. See Judith Bonner, *"Arts and Letters:* An Illustrated Periodical of Nineteenth Century New Orleans," *The Southern Quarterly,* xxvii, no. 2 (Winter 1989): 59-76.

7. Grace King, *Memories of a Southern Woman of Letters* (New York: 1932), 49.

8. William H. Gerdts and Russell Burke, *American Still-Life Painting* (New York: 1971), 128.

9. George Washington Cable, *Old Creole Days* (New York: 196l), 16.

CHAPTER SEVEN

1. See Winslow Ames, *Prince Albert and Victorian Taste* (New York: 1968).

2. William R. Cullison III, "Two Southern Impressionists, An Exhibit of the Work of the Woodward Brothers, William and Ellsworth" (New Orleans: 1984), ix.

3. Helen Gardner, *Art Through the Ages* (New York: 1959), 662.

4. William H. Gerdts, *Revealed Masters: 19th Century American Art* (New York: 1974), 37.

5. Rick Stewart, "Toward a New South: The Regionalist Approach, 1909-1950," in *Painting in the South* (Richmond: 1983), 106.

6. Donald Keyes, *Impressionism and the South* (Greenville, S.C.: 1988), 16.

7. See Estill Curtis Pennington, *Catherine Wiley: Genteel Southern Impressionist* (Nashville: 1990).

8. Thomas Nelson Page, *The Old South* (New York: 1919), 253.

9. Novak, *American Painting of the Nineteenth Century,* 243.

10. Michelle Favrot Heidelberg, "William Woodward" (diss., Tulane University, 1974), 29.

11. See Works Progress Administration, *New Orleans Artists Directory* (New Orleans Museum of Art).

12. Ellsworth Woodward, "The Magic of New Orleans," unpublished lecture, Ellsworth Woodward files, New Orleans Museum of Art.

13. Suzanne Ormond and Mary E. Irvine, *Louisiana's Art Nouveau: The Crafts of the Newcomb Style* (Gretna, La.: Pelican Publishing Company, 1976), 116.

14. Ellsworth Woodward, "The Purpose in Art Teaching," unpublished lecture, Ellsworth Woodward files, New Orleans Museum of Art.

15. Ellsworth Woodward, "The South Today," unpublished lecture, Ellsworth Woodward file, New Orleans Museum of Art.

CHAPTER EIGHT

1. Prescott N. Dunbar, *The New Orleans Museum of Art: The First Seventy-Five Years* (Baton Rouge: 1990), 47-48.

2. For a complete record of exhibitions at the New Orleans Museum of Art, see the list compiled by Valerie Loupe Olson in the chief curator's office at the museum.

3. See David F. Burg, *The White City* (Lexington, Ky.: 1973).

4. Lewis Hoyer Rabbage, *Helen H. Turner, N.A.* (Cragsmoor, N.Y.: 1983), 9.

5. See the papers of the Arts and Crafts Club, Historic New Orleans Collection.

6. Robert Hughes, *The Shock of the New* (New York: 1981), 9.

7. See Jessie Poesch, *Will Henry Stevens* (Greenville, S.C.: 1987) and, by the same author, "Will Henry Stevens, Modern Mystic: Beginnings to 1921," *The Southern Quarterly,* xxv (Fall 1986): 57-71.

8. Eleanor Early, "Gave Up the Most Beautiful Model in Paris for Art on a Tropic Isle," *EveryWeek Magazine* (1930), unpaged.

9. See Kathleen Orillion, *Paul Ninas* (Baton Rouge: 1986).

10. See Wanda M. Corn, *Grant Wood: The Regionalist Vision* (New Haven: 1983).

11. Thomas Craven, *A Treasury of American Prints* (New York: 1939), i.

12. Richard Cox et al., *Louisiana*

Images (Baton Rouge: 1980), unpaged.

13. See Kathleen Orillion, *Conrad Albrizio* (Baton Rouge: 1986).

14. See Redding Sugg, Jr., ed., *The Horn Island Logs of Walter Anderson* (Memphis: 1973).

15. The typescript of Walter Anderson's journal from the 1943 trip to New Orleans is now in the possession of the Walter Anderson estate, Ocean Springs, Mississippi.

16. See Estill Curtis Pennington, "Walter Anderson in New Orleans," *Arts Quarterly,* x, no. 3 (New Orleans Museum of Art: July/August/September 1988):5-9.

Designed by Dana Bilbray and Tracey Clements.
Composed in Garamond by Printech Desktop Publishing.
Four-color separations by Dai Nippon Printing Co., Ltd.
Printed on 113 gsm S-Lite Japan matte art paper by Roland Ultra RUU-5 and bound in Hi-Scarf by Buckram by Dai Nippon Printing Co., Ltd.

Ellsworth Woodward (1861-1939)
The Hearth, circa 1900
gouache on paper
10 x 14 inches
Roger Houston Ogden Collection, New Orleans

INDEX